MiG-23/27

Flogger in action

By Hans-Heiri Stapfer

Color by Don Greer
Illustrated by Perry Manley

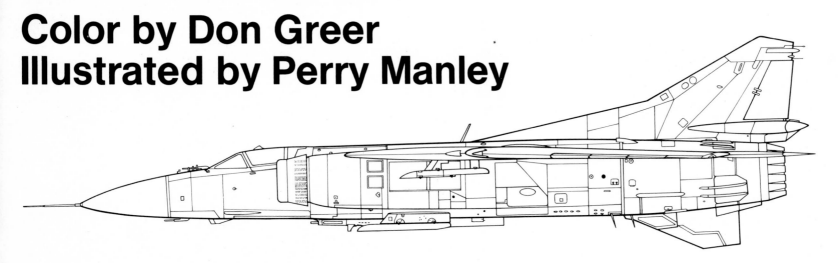

Aircraft Number 101
squadron/signal publications

A pair of Lybian Arab Air Force MiG-23 Floggers from Al Bumbah Air Base aggressively confront a flight of F-14 Tomcats from the USS JOHN F. KENNEDY over the Mediterranean Sea on 4 January 1989. A few minutes later, both Floggers were shot down by air-to-air missiles fired by the Tomcats.

ISBN 0-89747-244-6

If you have any photographs of the aircraft, armor, soldiers or ships of any nation, particularly wartime snapshots, why not share them with us and help make Squadron/Signal's books all the more interesting and complete in the future. Any photograph sent to us will be copied and the original returned. The donor will be fully credited for any photos used. Please send them to:

Squadron/Signal Publications, Inc.
1115 Crowley Drive.
Carrollton, TX 75011-5010.

PHOTO CREDITS

U.S. Navy	Robert Gretzyngier
Soldat und Technik	Karl Hanggi
Polish Air Force	D. D. Photo Service
Walter Hodel	Wojciech Luczak
U.S. Department of Defense	M.T.I. Interfoto
Guther Lippert	Hannu Valtonen
Martin Kyburz	Nicholas J. Waters III
Urs Harnisch	The Red Baron

DEDICATON

To a blonde enigma named Evelyne, or can you call it stupidity if you always fall in love at the wrong time with the wrong girl.

Besides the Soviet Air Force, the MiG-23 Flogger is used by a number of other countries. This pair of MiG-23 Flogger Gs of the East German Air Force are based at Peenemünde on the Baltic Sea.

INTRODUCTION

Today the MiG-23/27 Flogger series equips more Soviet fighter and attack regiments than any other Soviet fighter in service. In Europe, there are an estimated one thousand Floggers (in both Soviet and WARSAW Pact service) deployed opposite NATO forces. The MiG-23 was the first swing wing aircraft built by the MiG OKB and over the years the Flogger has proven itself to be a simple and reliable aircraft, serving in both the fighter and attack role.

The roots of the MiG-23's variable geometry or swing wing design date back to the early 1960s when a number of countries were investigating the merits of the variable geometry wing. The swing wing had been recognized by the MiG OKB as the best way of overcoming the primary shortcomings of the MiG-21 Fishbed fighter; i.e., short range and small weapons load. Fully spread, the swing wing offered a shorter takeoff/landing roll while carrying a heavier weapons load. In the fully swept position, the wing allowed for a high top speed and good supersonic handling characteristics.

The swing wing, however, also had some disadvantages. The construction of the wing sweep mechanism required a larger fuselage and is relatively heavy. Additionally, the variable wing and its mechanism places a higher demand on maintenance crews.

The Soviet Union was not the only country that appreciated the advantages of a swing wing fighter. In England, Vickers-Armstrongs had designed a practical swing wing aircraft. The British government, however, had no interest in such a project and all research data was transferred to the United States National Air and Space Administration's (NASA) Langley Research Center.

This data was instrumental in the early development of the General Dynamics TFX project, which evolved into the F-111. Since the beginning of the Cold War, the Soviets had tried to obtain information, documents, research data and hardware on new American projects through both official and unofficial channels and the TFX/F-111 project was no exception.

All research data obtained on the TFX project was carefully examined by Soviet aeronautical engineers, including those at the Central Aerodynamics and Hydrodynamics Institute (TsAGI) in Moscow where substantial research work on a Soviet swing wing fighter had already been done. This data, both that obtained on the TFX project and the original Soviet research data, was provided to the Sukhoi and MiG OKBs for use in developing new fighter projects. These projects were not in competition with each other and were aimed at totally different requirements. While Sukhoi's goal was to improve the takeoff/landing performance of the Su-7 Fitter ground attack series, the MiG OKB's goal was to design a completely new interceptor/fighter series.

MiG's project was much more radical. The new fighter was to be a replacement for the MiG-21 Fishbed with greatly improved range, weapons load and better takeoff/landing capabilities, establishing a new trend in the Soviet Union toward multi-role aircraft.

Not quite sure if the swing wing project would be a success, the MiG OKB also developed a delta winged prototype using roughly the same fuselage. The parallel development of two different wing configurations is quite common in the Soviet Union and both designs were taken to the prototype stage during 1966, roughly six years after the swing wing project was first discussed in Moscow.

The MiG-23DPD Faithless prototype on final approach for landing at the Ramenskoye flight test center. One Faithless STOL prototype was built and it was evaluated alongside the swing wing MiG-23I Flogger prototype.

MiG-23DPD Faithless

The parallel development to the swing wing fighter prototype was known as the MiG-23DPD. Although it has been widely reported that this aircraft was known as the Ye-23UVP, recent research reveals that the MiG-21 series was the last to use the Ye bureau numbers to designate prototypes. The most radical feature of the MiG-23DPD was the installation of an engine bay in the center fuselage, housing two forward inclined Koliesov lift engines mounted in tandem. These engines provided lift for takeoff and landing. The lift engines were provided with a rear-hinged and louvered door type intake on the top of the fuselage and exhausted through a grid of pilot controlled transverse louvers on the fuselage underside.

The idea of the jet-lift fighter was initiated by A.N. Rafaelyants during 1957 and the configuration had been tested with the MiG-21DPD. A number of proven components from the Fishbed had been used in the construction of the MiG-23DPD, including the wing shape and the main landing gear. All MiG designs built up to that time had the engine air intake located in the nose; however, the MiG-23DPD had the intake relocated to alongside the cockpit to make room in the nose for a radar antenna.

The MiG-23DPD was powered by a single 22,046 lbst Lyulka AL-7F turbojet engine, the same engine used in the Su-7 Fitter. Although reliable, it had a high fuel consumption.

The MiG-23DPD flew for the first time during April of 1967 in competition with the MiG-23I, the swing wing fighter prototype. Initial flight testing of both aircraft was made by the OKB test pilots, followed by a series of tests flown by the LII-GA (Flight Experimental Institute of Civil Aviation) which is responsible for testing all new designs, both military and civil. All testing was done at the Test and Experimental base at Ramenskoye. After successful completion of testing by the LII-GA, the prototype is then passed to the NIIVVSRKKA, the Science and Experimental Institute of the Air Force, which makes the final decision on production for the Soviet Air Force.

The trials clearly showed the advantages of the MiG-23I over the MiG-23DPD. The two lift engines in the fuselage reduced the aircraft's internal fuel capacity, used large quantities of fuel on takeoff and landing, dramatically reducing the aircraft's range and they could not be used in level flight.

The MiG-23DPD was demonstrated to the public by Pyotr Ostapenko on Aviation Day, 9 July 1967, at Domodedovo airfield. As a result of this demonstration, the aircraft was assigned the NATO reporting name Faithless.

Both the MiG-21DPD and MiG-23DPD proved to be less than successful and neither aircraft was developed beyond the prototype stage.

MiG-23I

The swing wing fighter prototype proved to be quite a demanding undertaking for the MiG OKB. While much of the basic research data on swing wings was provided by the TsAGI, a considerable design effort was required to mate this wing to a usable fighter fuselage. This effort was headed up by Rostislav Belyakov.

The swing wing's design showed a remarkable similarity to that of the American F-111, but with a marginally smaller wing sweep angle and more widely spaced pivot points. The wing had three sweep settings, 17 degrees, 45 degrees and 71 degrees. The wing control was manual and took approximately fifteen seconds to fully sweep the wing from the forward position to the fully swept back position. The wings had full span, three segment, trailing edge flaps and overwing spoilers, but no ailerons. Roll control is accomplished by the all flying horizontal stabilizers, which can be operated together to control pitch or separately to control roll. Each stabilizer is driven by a large electrohydraulic power unit. This type of control surface has come to be known in the West by the term — taileron.

While the MiG-23DPD had been equipped with a small centerline ventral fin similar to that used on the MiG-21 Fishbed, the MiG-23I had a large ventral fin which was hinged to fold to starboard when the landing gear was lowered.

While the MiG-23DPD Faithless had a landing gear adopted from the MiG-21 Fishbed, an entirely new design was introduced on the MiG-23I. In the lowered position, the main landing gear legs are horizontal with the wheels mounted on trailing arms that keep the wheel in the vertical. The legs are pivoted at the inner end, close to the centerline of the aircraft. Upon retraction the main leg is pulled straight up and slightly to the rear by the vertical retraction jack. The trailing arm folds downward and forward until the wheel is stowed almost horizontal in the wheel well located in the underside of the fuselage. The well is closed over by doors on the top and bottom of the well and on the gear legs. One of the landing gear well doors also doubles as a debris guard which covers the main gear wheel when the gear is down.

The MiG-23I was powered by a 22,046 lbst Lyulka AL-7F turbojet engine mounted in the rear of the semi-monocoque fuselage. The fuselage has a circular cross section, flattened along the cockpit sides in front of the air intakes. The vertical movable ramp air intakes on the MiG-23I prototype were quite similar to those used on the McDonnell Douglas F-4 Phantom. To admit extra airflow for the engine at low speeds, a pair of rectangular blow-in auxiliary doors are provided on each inlet under the wing glove.

The MiG-23I prototype (I stands for variable) flew for the first time during April of 1967. Together with the MiG-23DPD prototype, it was demonstrated for the first time on Aviation Day at Domodedovo, being flown by Aleksandr Fedotov. NATO assigned the reporting name Flogger to the prototype, although at the time NATO officials had no indication of the aircraft's builder or actual Soviet designation.

The first MiG-23I prototype carried the tactical number Blue 231 on the nose and was followed by at least nine other prototypes. The first and third prototypes are on perma-

Blue 231 was the first MiG-23I Flogger A prototype. The aircraft made its first flight during April of 1967 and was tested at Ramenskoye alongside the Faithless prototype.

nent exhibit in the Air Force Museum at Monino, near Moscow.

Trials with both prototypes clearly showed the advantages of the swing wing fighter over the lift engine prototype. The MiG-23DPD project was cancelled, while the Soviets ordered the MiG-23I into production during 1969, initially with an order for a number of pre-production aircraft to equip an operational test and evaluation squadron.

The Flogger A prototype makes a low pass over Ramenskoye during its flight test program. A total of ten MiG-23I prototypes were built and tested. The first prototype was preserved and is now on display at the Air Force Museum at Monino.

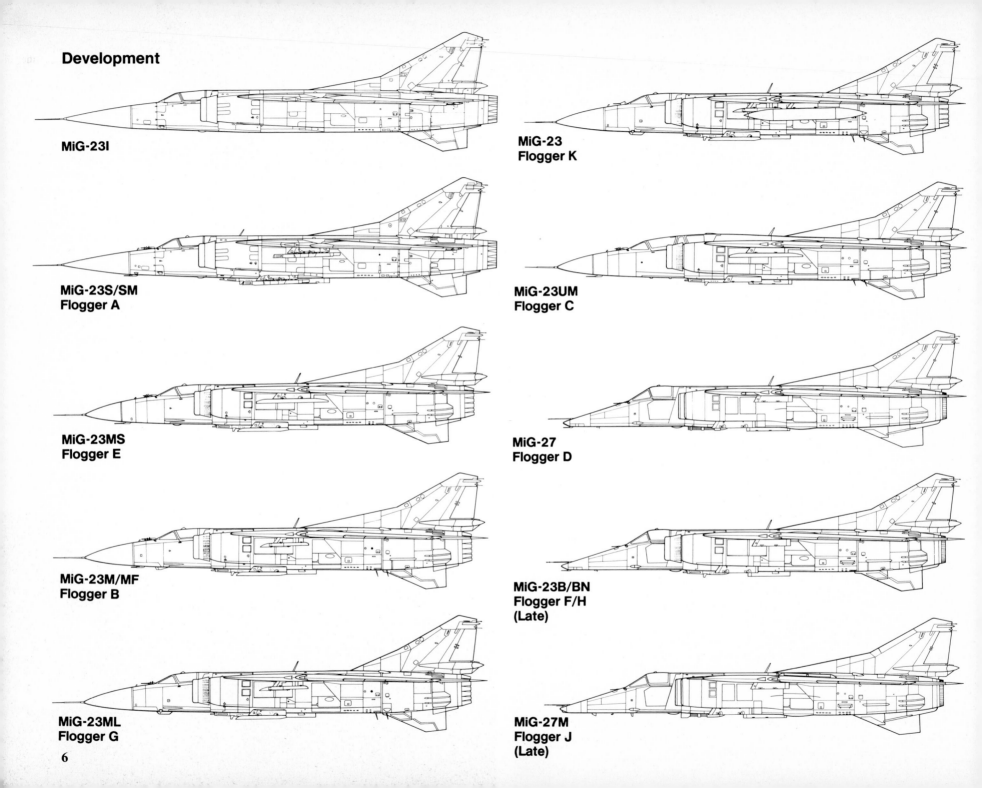

Development

MiG-23I

MiG-23S/SM
Flogger A

MiG-23MS
Flogger E

MiG-23M/MF
Flogger B

MiG-23ML
Flogger G

MiG-23
Flogger K

MiG-23UM
Flogger C

MiG-27
Flogger D

MiG-23B/BN
Flogger F/H
(Late)

MiG-27M
Flogger J
(Late)

6

MiG-23S/SM FLOGGER A

During 1969, the Soviet Air Force ordered a small production batch of some 100 MiG-23I aircraft under the service designation MiG-23S, allocating the aircraft to an evaluation unit for service testing under operational conditions. Soviet pilots quickly found that the MiG-23S was far different than the delta winged MiG-21 Fishbeds they had been flying. The MiG-23S had twice the engine thrust of the MiG-21, twice the internal fuel and more than twice the gross weight.

As it became apparent in the West that the swing wing MiG-23 fighter had entered production and was being produced in quantity, NATO assigned the reporting name Flogger A to these early production variants.

The MiG-23S differed from the MiG-23I in a number of ways. While the prototypes carried no weapons or radar, the MiG-23S was fully equipped for combat missions. An S-21 Saphir air search radar (called Jay Bird by NATO) was installed in the nose giving the Flogger A a limited all weather capability. Internal armament consisted of a GSh-23L twin barreled 23MM cannon mounted in a semi-recessed housing on the fuselage centerline. The weapon was installed in such a manner that the entire gun housing could be lowered from the fuselage by means of an internal winch, which greatly eased maintenance and rearming. The cannon weighed 114 pounds and had a rate of fire of 3,400 rounds per minute. To achieve this high rate of fire, the cannon utilizes the Gast principle (originally developed in Germany during 1916) in which the recoil of one cannon automatically loads and fires the second cannon. The GSh-23L has proven to be a very reliable weapon.

Externally the MiG-23S carries four ordnance pylons, two under the fuselage and one under each wing glove. These pylons could be fitted with launcher shoes for air-to-air missiles or with bombs/rocket pods. The standard air-to-air missile carried by the MiG-23S was the K-13A (AA-2 Atoll). This weapon was a Soviet copy of the American AIM-9B Sidewinder. Early K-13s were rather unreliable and followed anything — but the intended target. The AA-2 Atoll has been progressively improved over the years and is now regarded as a reliable air-to-air missile. A tear drop shaped antenna was installed on the starboard wing pylon.

In addition to the ordnance pylons, a centerline fuselage pylon was fitted to the MiG-23S which was used to carry a 176 gallon external fuel tank.

MiG-23S avionics including an SP-50 ILS system, with the antenna mounted on the underside of the nose just behind the radome, a three pole SRO-2 IFF system (called Odd Rods by NATO) installed on the nose just ahead of the canopy and a VHF blade antenna for the RSIU-5 radio on the dorsal spine behind the canopy. To improve the pilot's rear view, an electrically heated rear view mirror was installed in the upper canopy.

While neither the MiG-23DPD or MiG-23I prototypes were equipped with speed brakes, the MiG-23S had four small speed brakes installed on the tail just ahead of the engine exhaust. The brakes were mounted above and below the horizontal stabilizer and when viewed from the front, formed an X when deployed.

The MiG-23S was followed into service by an improved variant, the MiG-23SM (M stands for modified). The changes between the MiG-23S and MiG-23SM were mainly internal and resulted from requirements dictated by the operational testing of the MiG-23S. The first MiG-23SMs were delivered during late 1969 and, although the MiG-23SM was a sound design, a decision had been reached to replace the Lyulka engine with a lighter, more powerful, and more fuel efficient Tumansky R-27 turbojet. As result, production of the MiG-23S/SM was held to a very limited number.

As soon as the Tumansky powered variants became available, the MiG-23S/SMs were withdrawn from service. These aircraft were not exported and, in fact, were never

This MiG-23SM Flogger A, Yellow 20, is painted in an air superiority Gray camouflage and is configured with four K-13 (AA-2) Atoll air-to-air missile rails on the wing and under fuselage pylons. The radome, fin cap, and ventral fin leading edge are in White.

used outside the Soviet Union. The very short operational life of the MiG-23SM was not because of any technical shortcomings in the basic design, it was simply because a better powerplant had become available to replace the heavy and "thirsty" Lyulka engine.

This preserved Flogger is one of the early Lyulka powered MiG-23S Flogger As. The aircraft was repainted for this display and carries a non-standard camouflage scheme and national insignia.

MiG-23MS FLOGGER E

While the MiG-23S/SMs were being introduced into service, the MiG OKB was working on re-engining the MiG-23 airframe with the 22,485 lbst Tumansky R-27-300 turbojet. This engine had been developed by Sergei Konstantinovich Tumanski and his staff some eight years after the Lyulka AL-7F-1 engine and therefore benefited from newer engine technololgy.

The R-27-300 was one foot shorter and slightly lighter than the AL-7F-1, was much more fuel efficient and was much more responsive to the throttle, going from idle to full afterburner in 4.5 seconds. It also did not emit the smoke trail that was common to the Lyulka engine. Unlike most western nations, the Soviet Union had elected to stay with the turbojet for its new generation of fighter aircraft, while most western aircraft were being powered by turbofan engines. Turbofan engines had several major drawbacks as far as the Soviets were concerned; they required more exotic materials in manufacture, a more sophisticated engine cooling system and had far greater maintenance demands.

The first trials with the Tumansky powered MiG-23 begun during 1969, three years after the MiG-23I prototype had made its first flight. Given the designation MiG-23MS, the aircraft also underwent a number of aerodynamic changes brought about by the installation of the new engine. While the overall length of the aircraft was not changed, the horizontal stabilizers were relocated some two feet to the rear and the engine after-burner nozzle was shortened. This gave the MiG-23MS increased maneuverability by a reduction in the aircraft's natural stability and an increase in control authority.

Retaining the original overall span, the wing was modified by a 20 percent increase in chord at the root and tip of the movable wing panel. The extended portion of the wing panel terminated in what might be described as a "claw" immediately outboard of the fixed wing glove. This gave the wing a dogtooth at the intermediate sweep angle.

These changes had a number of beneficial effects. The forward movement of the aerodynamic center combined with the rear movement of the tail surfaces served to increase overall control effectiveness and maneuverability. The increased taper of the pivoting wing panels reduced the aerodynamic shift that occurred with changes in the wing sweep. The wing dogtooth created a powerful vortex which re-energies the airflow at high angles of attack and maintained maximum spoiler effectiveness, again increasing maneuverability.

The radome on the MiG-23MS differed from the MiG-23S/SM in being shorter and wider, although it still housed a Jay Bird radar. A blister, housing a Doppler navigation antenna, was added to the port side of the nose, the ILS antenna was repositioned slightly forward on the underside of the nose and a yaw vane was added to the top of the nose just to the rear of the radome. The VHF radio antenna mast was also repositioned, being moved rearward on the fuselage spine.

The air intake was redesigned, being deeper and having a more angled opening. A single air pressure probe was added to the lower portion of the portside air intake, while two air pressure probes were added at the same position on the starboard side. These probes served as pressure sensors for the automatic air intake control system.

The MiG-23MS featured a KM-1 ejection seat. This seat can be used at speeds up to 745 mph and at altitudes up to 75,000 feet. It is rated as a zero-zero seat, although on the ground the aircraft must have a forward speed of at least 80 mph before an ejection can be successfully initiated. The seat includes a KP-27M oxygen system and a NAZ-7 emergency survival kit. The KM-1 seat is the standard ejection seat used for all Flogger variants and is also used on a number of other MiG fighters including the MiG-25 Foxbat. The KM-1 seat is widely disliked by MiG-23 pilots because of its tendency to cause back injuries during ejection. Whenever possible, MiG-23 pilots will crash land rather than eject.

A Soviet Air Force MiG-23MS Flogger E taxis out on a snow covered airfield. The Flogger E used the S-21 Saphir air intercept radar adopted from the Jay Bird radar used on late production MiG-21 Fishbeds.

Fuselage/Wing Development

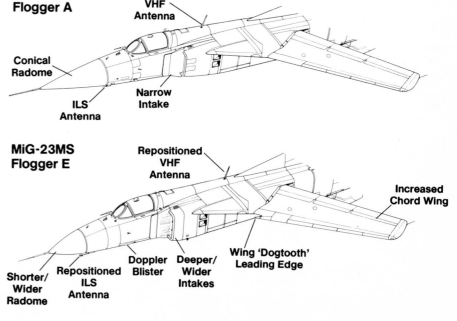

MiG-23S/SM Flogger A
VHF Antenna
Conical Radome
ILS Antenna
Narrow Intake

MiG-23MS Flogger E
Repositioned VHF Antenna
Increased Chord Wing
Shorter/Wider Radome
Repositioned ILS Antenna
Doppler Blister
Deeper/Wider Intakes
Wing 'Dogtooth' Leading Edge

The rear fuselage air brakes were changed, being enlarged and strengthened with two external metal reinforcement bars. The external reinforcement allowed the speed brakes to be employed at higher speeds.

Flight tests of the Tumansky powered MiG-23MS were quite favorable and the advantages of the R-27-300 powerplant along with the aerodynamic refinements of the MiG-23 airframe convinced the Soviets to order the type into production, with the examples becoming operational during 1971.

The MiG-23MS, however, was viewed by the Soviets as an interim interceptor/fighter and the number assigned to Soviet fighter regiments was fairly small. While the MiG-23MS was entering service, the MiG OKB was already working on a variant with more sophisticated electronics and an greatly improved radar system. The few MiG-23MS fighters that actually entered Soviet service had a brief life and Soviet squadrons that operated the type were never deployed outside the Soviet Union.

A number of these early MiG-23MS Floggers Es were exported to Algeria, Egypt, Lybia, Iraq and Syria. It must be noted that the Flogger was exported to these countries in the Middle East long before any of the countries in the WARSAW Pact were equipped with the MiG-23 and none of the WARSAW Pact countries were ever equipped with the MiG-23MS. The first MiG-23MS fighters that were exported went to the Middle East during 1974.

Although the MiG-23MS was developed before later MiG-23 fighter variants, it carries a NATO reporting name suffix later than the aircraft that followed it into service. This was because NATO did not become aware of the aircraft until after it had sighted the follow-on variants in Soviet service. Thus, when the MiG-23MS was first sighted in Libya during 1974, it was assumed to be a new variant and assigned the NATO reporting name Flogger E. In fact, NATO (and others) assumed the aircraft was a dedicated export variant of the later Flogger fighter variants and not an older aircraft.

One reason for this mix-up was that the MiG-23MS was equipped with the Jay Bird radar. The Jay Bird had a search range of 18 miles and a tracking range of 12 miles. During the early 1970s, the Soviets did not want to export their new technology radars and found the early MiG-23MS with the Jay Bird to be perfect for export to their Middle East clients. Additionally, the Jay Bird equipped MiG-23MS could easily be absorbed by the receiving air forces because most had been or were flying late model MiG-21s also equipped with the Jay Bird.

During 1982, the Syrian Air Force introduced the MiG-23MS into combat against Israeli F-16s over the Bekaa Valley, in Lebanon. Within a week, the Syrians had lost over eighty aircraft (at least thirty-six Floggers) while the IDF/AF lost two aircraft.

In Lybia, the MiG-23MS became the back-bone of the Lybian Arab Air Force. Initially the Floggers were painted with a Red/White/Black roundel. Later, COL Muammar el-Gadaffi ordered that the roundel be replaced by a simple Green dot, the color of Islam.

The MiG-23MS Flogger E was widely, exported with Libya being one of the first countries in the Middle East to receive the Flogger. This Libyan Flogger, Black 6916, is armed with four AA-2 Atoll air-to-air missiles and carries Western style numbers on the starboard side of the aircraft and Arabic style numbers on the port side.

Over the years Lybian MiG-23MS Flogger Es have been active in combat against Chad and Egypt. In at least two incidents, Lybian pilots defected with their MiG-23s, one of these crashing in Italy and another landing on Crete. On 1 March 1988 four MiG-23s landed in Egypt reportedly due to a fuel shortage and all four aircraft returned to Lybia two days later.

On 4 January 1989 two Lybian Floggers took off from al Bumbah Air Base. The two were vectored against two F-14 Tomcats operating from the USS JOHN F. KENNEDY some seventy miles north of the Libyan coast, After repeated attempts to shake the Floggers failed and receiving indications that the MiG-23s had turned on their fire control radar, the F-14s finally declared the two Lybians as hostile and engaged. One MiG-23 was shot down by a Sparrow launched by the F-14 wingman, while the second was destroyed by a Sidewinder launched by the F-14 leader.

The sole operator of the MiG-23MS in the Americas is the Cuban Fuerza Aerea Revolucionaria, which has a force of about twenty Flogger Es based at San Julian in the air defense role.

Yellow 85, a MiG-23MS Flogger E of a Soviet Frontal Aviation unit, taxies out to begin another sortie. The Flogger E actually preceded the Flogger B into service; however, the aircraft was not detected by NATO until after it had been exported, which was long after the later Flogger Bs were already in service.

Rear Fuselage Development

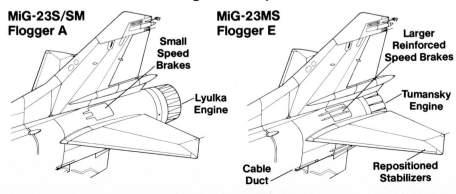

MiG-23S/SM Flogger A
Small Speed Brakes
Lyulka Engine

MiG-23MS Flogger E
Larger Reinforced Speed Brakes
Tumansky Engine
Cable Duct
Repositioned Stabilizers

9

MiG-23M/MF FLOGGER B

Shortly after the MiG-23MS entered production and squadron service, the Soviets completed development of an improved air intercept radar and it was decided that this radar should be installed in a Flogger airframe as quickly as possible.

The radar was broadly comparable to the American-built Westinghouse AWG-10 used in the McDonnell Douglas F-4J Phantom II, both in size and operation. It has a mechanically steered scanner approximately twenty-six inches in diameter, operates in the J-band and works on the pulse Doppler principle for search and track. The radar's range in the search mode is about 50 miles while range in the track mode is 35 miles. Given the NATO reporting name High Lark, the radar would allow the Flogger to carry a beyond-visual-range (BVR), radar guided air-to-air missile. The missile selected for use on the MiG-23 was the R-23 (NATO reporting name AA-7 Apex) the first Soviet missile designed to be used for BVR attacks against fighter sized targets.

The new Flogger variant, designated the MiG-23M, was the first Soviet fighter to feature a genuine all weather, beyond visual range kill capability and the first Soviet fighter capable of tracking targets flying below its own altitude (although the High Lark cannot guide a missile to a low flying target). The main external difference between the MiG-23MS and MiG-23M was a much larger fiberglass radome for the High Lark antenna. The MiG-23M was also equipped with an improved Doppler navigation system with the antenna being mounted on the underside of the nose just behind the radome, and a TP-23 IR sensor which is carried in a housing under the nose in front of the nose wheel well.

There were a number of other differences between the MiG-23MS and MiG-23M. The ILS antenna was offset to the port side of the nose, the avionics bay cooling air scoops on the side of the nose were relocated, being moved slightly higher and to the rear and the yaw vane on top of the nose was also moved to the rear. Early production MiG-23Ms adopted a number of features found on the earlier MiG-23MS (Flogger E), which were then changed on later production aircraft. Early production MiG-23Ms had no frame on the centerline of the canopy, while later production MiG-23Ms featured a frame running through the center of the canopy (which also enclosed the electrically heated rear view mirror housing).

Red 24 was the prototype for the MiG-23M Flogger B. The Flogger B differed from the earlier MiG-23MS Flogger E in a number of ways including a much larger radar and radome, modified weapons pylons, and additional avionics and sensors.

Late production MiG-23Ms featured trim tabs on the horizontal stabilizers and the power assisted rudder was strengthened by the addition of a second hinge. The MiG-23M also featured an enlarged and different shaped wing glove missile pylon. The new pylon had more space between the pylon and the wing undersurface to accommodate the large R-23 (AA-7 Apex) air-to-air missile.

Avionics installed in the MiG-23M include a R-832M UHF radio, an ARL-S data link transever, an ARK-15M radio compass, a MRP-56P navigation beacon receiver, a RSBN-6S short range navigation system, and a RW-4 radio altimeter. A full electronics warfare system is also installed including Sirena S-3M tail warning radar, wing and tail mounted SRO-69 Radar Warning Receiver (RWR) antennas and an SRO-2M Odd Rods IFF system.

Another major change between the MiG-23MS and the MiG-23M was the powerplant. The MiG-23M replaced the earlier 22,485 lbst R-27-300 engine with a more powerful 27,500 lbst Tumansky R-29B engine. The internal fuel capacity was also increased, with additional fuel cells being installed in the outer wing panels and flexible cells being installed in the fuselage, for a total of 1,519 gallons. This internal fuel load can be augmented by a 176 gallon drop tank on the fuselage centerline station and two additional drop tanks on non-swiveling outboard wing pylons. These tanks, however, must be jettisioned before the wing can be fully swept back.

The MiG-23M is a counter-air fighter and is normally armed with two R-23 (AA-7 Apex) and two K-13 (AA-2 Atoll) or R-60 (AA-8 Aphid) air-to-air missiles, plus its internal gun. The long ranged R-23 (AA-7) Apex is available in two variants: the R-23T (infrared homing) and R-23R (semi-active radar homing). The R-23 was developed during the early 1970s and has been described as the Soviet equivalent to the American AIM-7 Sparrow. It has a length of 15 feet 1 ¼ inches, weighs 705 pounds (of which 80 pounds is warhead), has a range of twenty miles and a speed of nearly Mach 3.

The short range R-60 (AA-8 Aphid) is rapidly replacing the aging AA-2 Atoll series of missiles as the standard Soviet IR guided weapon. With a length of 7 feet 2 ½ inches, it is one of the smallest air-to-air missiles in service with any country. The R-60 weighs approximately 121 pounds, with a 13.2 pound warhead, has a speed of Mach 2.5 and a range of approximately five miles. It was first observed by the West during 1976 and by

This camouflaged, early production MiG-23M Flogger B carries twin AA-8 Aphid missile rails on the wing glove pylon and a K-13 (AA-2) Atoll missile rail on the starboard under fuselage pylon.

the mid-1980s it had become the Soviet's standard short ranged air-to-air missile. To increase the fire power of the MiG-23M (and other platforms that carry AA-8s) the Soviets have developed a dual missile launcher rail capable of carrying two AA-8s and being mounted on any standard pylon that was capable of handling single AA-8 launcher rails.

The MiG-23M can also be used in a secondary ground attack role. For the air-to-ground mission the MiG-23M can be armed with UB-16 and UB-32 rocket pods. A special four bomb rack designed for carrying four FAB 100 bombs can also be carried on the wing and fuselage pylons. In addition a wide variety of standard Soviet bombs can be carried.

By the end of 1974, MiG-23M production had reached and exceeded four aircraft per week and over the next two years this rate was more than doubled. Eventually, MiG-23M production reached a point where some four hundred aircraft were being built annually.

The MiG-23M was first observed by the West when the aircraft was deployed to the German Democratic Republic as part of the Soviet Air Forces assigned to the Group of Soviet Forces in Germany (GSFG) during 1973 and NATO assigned the aircraft the reporting name Flogger B. The MiG-23 Flogger quickly became the most numerically important aircraft in the inventory of the GSFG. Regiments of some forty-five Floggers each are based at the following GSFG bases; Finow, Damgarten, Kothen, Juterbog, Zerbst, Merseburg, and Falkenberg.

During 1978, the Soviets began equipping WARSAW Pact countries with the Flogger B under the export designation MiG-23MF. The first country to receive the Flogger B was Bulgaria, followed shortly by East Germany and Czechoslovakia. Bulgaria operates

These early production MiG-23M Flogger Bs lack the center frame on the canopy, which became standard on all later production interceptor/fighter variants. The object in the upper portion of the canopy is the housing for the rear view mirror.

Nose Development

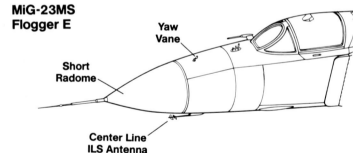

MiG-23MS Flogger E

- Yaw Vane
- Short Radome
- Center Line ILS Antenna

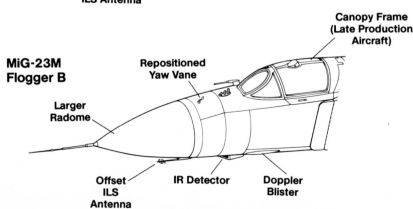

MiG-23M Flogger B

- Canopy Frame (Late Production Aircraft)
- Repositioned Yaw Vane
- Larger Radome
- Offset ILS Antenna
- IR Detector
- Doppler Blister

Red 458, a Polish Air Force MiG-23MF Flogger B, carries four AA-2 Atoll missile rails on the wing glove and fuselage pylons. This aircraft is a late production Flogger B with two hinges on the rudder.

Red 458, a Flogger B of the Polish Air Force, carries AA-2 Atoll missile rails on all four pylons. The aircraft is in the cruising configuration with the wing in the full forward position.

a regiment of forty MiG-23MFs, these aircraft carry three digit tactical numbers and are in air superiority Gray camouflage. East Germany operates forty-five aircraft assigned to *Jagdfliegergeschwader 9 Heinrich Rau* at Peenemünde on the Baltic Sea. The Czech Air Force operates flights of fifteen MiG-23MFs each as part of the air defense regiments under the 7th Air Defense Army. Flights are based at Bechyne, Plzen, with two flights based at Zatec. A Full regiment is based at Namesti Nad Oslanow. All Flogger depot level maintenance is carried out at Trencin. The Czech Air Force has at least 105 Flogger Bs currently in service.

The first Flogger Bs supplied to Poland were delivered during 1979. The Polish Air Force operates a single regiment of forty-five MiG-23MFs in the air defense role, based at Slupsk-Redzikowo. Until the summer of 1989, these aircraft were all camouflaged in an air superiority Gray with Red three digit tactical numbers. This has now changed with a number of aircraft being repainted with a tactical camouflage. Additionally, Polish Floggers are now sporting unit markings and the crest of the city where they are based.

Rumania has thirty-two MiG-23MFs based at Mihail-Kogalniceaunu Air Base as part of the Eastern Air Defense Division. A further sixteen MiG-23s, along with thirty-two MiG-21 Fishbeds, equip another fighter Regiment under the Western Air Defense Division.

The last WARSAW Pact country to be equipped with the MiG-23MF was Hungary where they were first revealed to the public during the Air Parade on 4 April 1980. There is one air defense regiment of thirty-five Flogger Bs based at Papa with additional Floggers based at Szolnok in the advanced training role. All Hungarian MiG-23MFs are painted in air superiority Gray with Red two digit tactical numbers. This number is not a part of the aircraft's serial number, as is the usual practice in WARSAW Pact nations, but is actually the number in which the aircraft entered service. Under this system, Red 05 is, in fact, the fifth Flogger B to enter service in Hungary.

Soviet pilots receive instructions before manning their MiG-23M Flogger Bs at a Soviet air base. The aircraft are early production Flogger Bs with AA-7 Apex missile rails on the wing pylons and AA-2 Atoll rails on the fuselage pylons.

Wing Glove Pylon

MiG-23MS Flogger E
MiG-23M Flogger B (Early)

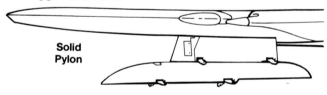

Solid Pylon

MiG-23M Flogger B (Late)

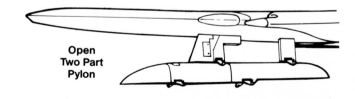

Open Two Part Pylon

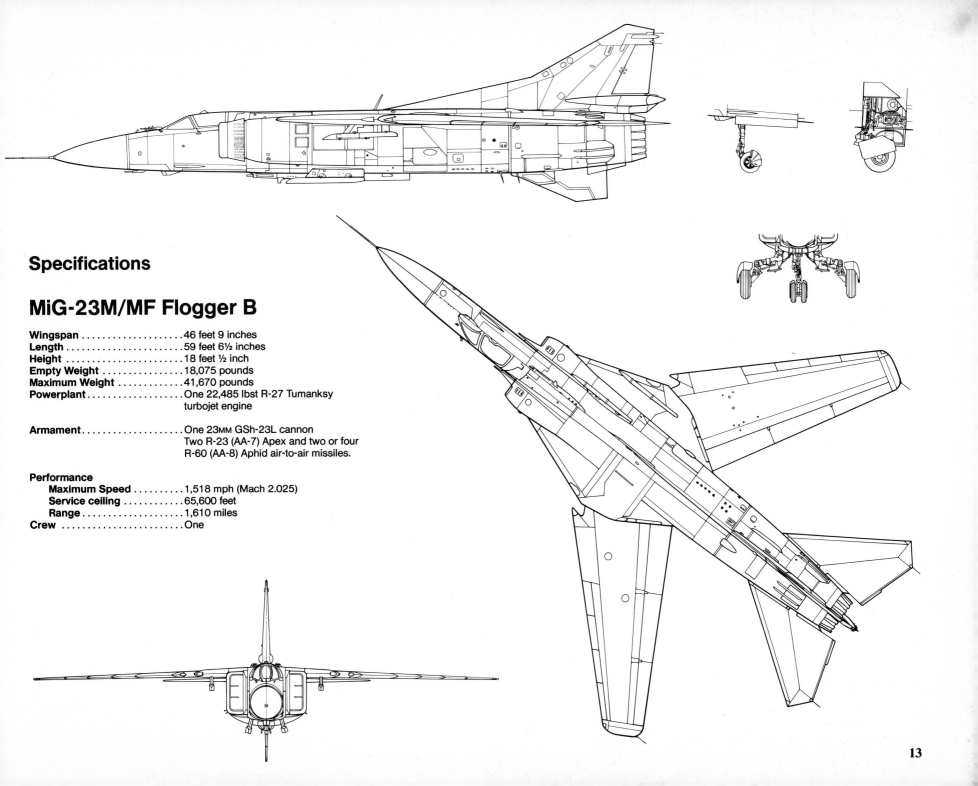

Specifications

MiG-23M/MF Flogger B

Wingspan .46 feet 9 inches
Length . . . . .59 feet 6½ inches
Height . . . . .18 feet ½ inch
Empty Weight . . . . .18,075 pounds
Maximum Weight . . . . .41,670 pounds
Powerplant . . . . .One 22,485 lbst R-27 Tumanksy
turbojet engine

Armament . . . . .One 23мм GSh-23L cannon
Two R-23 (AA-7) Apex and two or four
R-60 (AA-8) Aphid air-to-air missiles.

Performance
   Maximum Speed . . . . .1,518 mph (Mach 2.025)
   Service ceiling . . . . .65,600 feet
   Range .1,610 miles
Crew . . . . .One

The Flogger has had a high attrition rate in WARSAW Pact service. The MiG-23 is a demanding aircraft to fly and there were a number of losses traced to failure of the wing pivot mechanism. A common saying in WARSAW Pact countries is that the easiest way to obtain a MiG-23 is to purchase a piece of land and just wait.

A number of other countries have received MiG-23MF Flogger Bs including Syria, Angola, Iraq and India. The Syrians have suffered from a high number of operational losses, believed to be caused primarily by poor maintenance. Iraqi Air Force MiG-23s have seen combat in the Gulf war between Iraq and Iran. Besides the MiG-23MF Flogger B, Iraq also operates ground attack variants of the MiG-23 and it is believed that there are at least eighty Floggers (of all variants) in service with Iraq.

The Angolan Air Force operates some fifty-five Floggers, manned and maintained by Cuban pilots and ground crews. The first MiG-23s were received during 1985 and immediately deployed to the south of Angola to help defend against South African Air Force aircraft supporting UNITA (National Union for the Total Independence of Angola) in cross border raids. During late 1985, a Cuban flown Flogger was shot down while on a ground attack mission near the town of Maringa and the Cuban crew captured. In January of 1989 the Cubans began transferring the Floggers to Angolan pilots and started to withdraw their forces from Angola.

The prices paid by members of the WARSAW Pact for their Floggers varies from country to country. East Germany reportedly paid $3.6 million each, while the Czechs paid $6.6 million each. Each country must pay a percentage of this price in hard currency, except for the Czechs, who supply the Soviets with the L-39 Albatros trainer.

Red 10, a Hungarian Air Force MiG-23MF Flogger B, moves along the taxiway at Papa Air Base. The aircraft carries AA-7 Apex missile rails on the wing glove pylon and AA-2 Atoll rails on the fuselage pylons. The rear fuselage speed brakes are partially open.

A Czech Air Force MiG-23MF Flogger B is prepared for another sortie from Zatec Air Base. The Czech Air Force operates a number of Flogger B squadrons assigned to different air defense regiments under the 7th Air Defense Army.

Tail Development

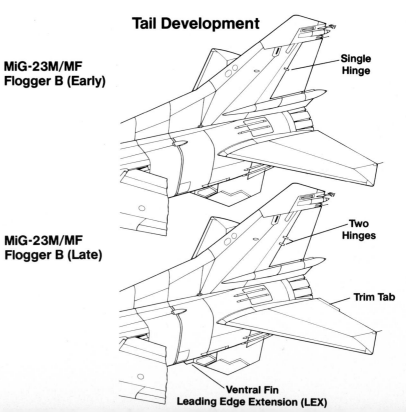

MiG-23M/MF
Flogger B (Early)

Single
Hinge

MiG-23M/MF
Flogger B (Late)

Two
Hinges

Trim Tab

Ventral Fin
Leading Edge Extension (LEX)

This early production MiG-23M Flogger B has a single hinge on the rudder and early style wing glove pylons fitted K-12 (AA-2) Atoll missile rails. The aircraft is painted in an overall air superiority Gray camouflage.

Ground crews receive their morning instructions in front of a line of Hungarian Air Force MiG-23MF Flogger Bs at Papa Air Base. All the aircraft have protective covers over the canopies, air intakes and blow-in doors.

Red 02, a Hungarian Air Force MiG-23MF, makes a low pass over Budaörs airfield during June of 1987. The aircraft has several patches of lighter Gray paint on the nose and tail where earlier markings have been painted over.

A MiG-23MF prepares to taxi out for a night training sortie. The retractable landing light on the port side intake duct is larger in diameter than the landing light under the starboard intake duct.

15

Polish technicians inspect the interior of the tail section of a Polish Air Force MiG-23MF Flogger B, Red 140. The entire tail section is removable to allow access to the engine and other components for maintenance.

Polish ground crews perform maintenance on Red 140, a MiG-23MF Flogger B. The tail section has been removed and the access panels that allow access to the engine driven hydraulic pumps are open.

A line-up of Polish MiG-23MF Flogger Bs at a Polish Air Base. Red 148, in the foreground, has a two color radome of Dark Green and White and carries AA-2 Atoll missile rails on both the wing and fuselage pylons. The next Flogger in the line, Red 117, carries AA-8 Aphid dual missile rails on the fuselage pylons.

Red 05, a MiG-23MF of the Hungarian Air Force, awaits the signal from the ground crewman to take its position on the runway. This same aircraft later crashed while training for the annual Air Parade air show conducted over Budapest.

These Flogger Bs are fitted with non-swiveling outer wing pylons and under wing fuel tanks used for long range missions. The wing tanks are not intended for use in combat, because the wing can not be swept back to its full back position with the tanks in place.

Ground crewmen work on Red 12, an overall air superiority Gray Hungarian Air Force MiG-23MF, on the flight line at Papa Air Base. The wire hanging on the ILS antenna is a communications lead which attaches to the ground crewman's helmet.

This Flogger B is in the long range ferry configuration and is fitted with three drop tanks, one under the fuselage and one under each wing. The wing pylons on the Flogger B do not swivel and the tanks must be jettisoned if the wing is swept back.

Red 591, a MiG-23MF Flogger B of the East German Air Force, takes off from Peenemünde Air Base armed with a pair UB-16 sixteen shot 57mm rocket pods on the fuselage pylon.

17

An East German Air Force MiG-23MF Flogger B rolls out on the runway with its braking parachute fully deployed. While early braking parachutes used on the Flogger were White, the parachutes now in service are White and Red.

A Hungarian Air Force MiG-23MF Flogger B, Red 02, makes a high speed pull up in full afterburner over Budaörs airfield during June of 1987. The aircraft carries two dual AA-8 Aphid missile rails on the fuselage pylons.

Red 591, a MiG-23MF of *Jagdfliegergeschwader 9 Heinrich Rau*, East German Air Force, takes off from Peenemüde Air Base. The wing is at the full forward position and the full span flaps are down. Peenemüde was the WWII launch site for the V-2 rocket attacks against London and Antwerp.

Red 564 of the East German Air Force departs from Peenemünde Air Base in full afterburner. The ventral fin is coming down into the vertical, in flight position as the landing gear is retracted.

This Polish Air Force MiG-23MF Flogger B, Red 120, is unusual for a WARSAW Pack fighter in that it carries unit insignias. The squadron insignia is painted on the nose and the crest of the city of Slupsk (where the unit is based) is on the air intake duct. (Wojciech Luczak)

Recently the Polish Air Force started painting their MiG-23's with the official crest of the city at which the aircraft are based. This MiG-23MF Flogger B has the crest of the city of Slupsk on the intake duct near the blow-in doors. (Wojciech Luczak)

This MiG-23MF Flogger B, Red 120, of the Polish Air Force carries the unit insignia of the Koszalin Air Defense Regiment on the nose. The aircraft is fitted with protective covers over the cockpit and infrared sensor housing under the fuselage.

Red 584, a MiG-23MF Flogger B of *Jagdfliegergeschwader 9 Heinrich Rau*, takes off from its home base at Peenemünde. This aircraft carries the winged "Q" maintenance award symbol on nose in front of the tactical number.

MiG-23ML FLOGGER G

During the early 1980s, the MiG OKB began a project to update the MiG-23M Flogger B with enhanced avionics and other improvements under the designation MiG-23ML. The first examples of this new Flogger were observed by the West at Rissala Air Base in Finland during a goodwill visit by a six aircraft detachment under the command of LTCOL J. Belenkov. The Soviets visited the Finnish MiG-21 Fishbed fighter unit at Rissala between 1 and 4 August 1978, giving western intelligence agencies their first good look at this new Flogger variant, which was assigned the NATO reporting name Flogger G.

Later that same year the same six MiG-23MLs visited the French Air Force Normandie-Niemen fighter unit at Rheims. This French unit had been formed in the Soviet Union during the Second World War and over the years a tradition of exchange visits between both countries was maintained. Later, Mirage F-1s of the Normandie-Niemen visited the Soviet Union. Finally, these same MiG-23MLs visited Sweden during mid-August of 1981. In all three visits, it was apparent that the Soviet pilots and ground crews had been thoroughly briefed for their exposure to the West.

The MiG-23MLs used for these visits were not standard Soviet front line aircraft and lacked several essential pieces of equipment, such as weapons pylons, IR detectors and some cockpit instrumentation. In addition, these six aircraft were all from a very early production block and had been specially prepared for trips to non-WARSAW Pact countries.

The standard MiG-23ML Flogger G differs from the earlier MiG-23M Flogger B in a number of ways. The most obvious difference is the reduced size of the dorsal fin in front of the vertical stabilizer. The small air intake found on the starboard side of the vertical stabilizer was deleted and the fuel line/electronic cable duct on the lower rear fuselage was also deleted.

Two small blisters were added to the rear fuselage just above the ventral fin (one on each side), replacing the single squared blister that was carried in front of the speed brake on the starboard side of the MiG-23M. These blisters house the lower hemisphere antennas of the Reper N electronic warfare system. The ventral fin was also modified with a small leading edge extension being added to the base of the fin and a small dielectric panel being added to the rear portion of the fixed portion of the fin.

The nose area of the MiG-23ML Flogger G was also modified. The nose wheel was strengthened with much larger torque scissors links being installed on the forward side of the nose wheel leg and larger tires being used. The shape of the TP-23 IR detector housing was changed and the ILS antenna was moved from the port to the starboard side of the nose. A new blade antenna was fitted to the underside of the nose on the port side of the IR detector housing. The small avionics bay air intake was also repositioned, being moved lower on the fuselage side.

Instead of a single angle of attack transmitter (located on the port side of the MiG-23M) the Flogger G was fitted with an angle of attack transmitter on both sides of the nose, somewhat lower than on the MiG-23M. The SRO-2M Odd Rods IFF antenna array was relocated further back on the nose, closer to the windscreen. The small air temperature probe fitted to the nose of the MiG-23M Flogger B, just in front of the windscreen, was deleted on the MiG-23ML (except for the six demonstration aircraft).

The positioning of the air pressure sensor tubes on the lower portion of the air intakes was reversed on the MiG-23ML; that is, instead of two sensors on the starboard side and one on the port side, (MiG-23M) two were now carried on the port side and one on the starboard side. On both variants (MiG-23M and ML) the retractable landing lights mounted on the underside of the air intake trunks vary in size, with the starboard light being larger than the port light.

Both the MiG-23MS (Flogger E) and MiG-23M (Flogger B) had internal strong points and external mounting points for a weapons pylon on the underside of each air intake duct. In the event, the pylons were rarely, if ever, used and the internal provision for these pylons was deleted on the MiG-23ML Flogger G.

The MiG-23ML Flogger G was first unveiled to the West when a detachment from Kubinka Air Base visited Rissala Air Base in Finland, during early August of 1978. The aircraft lacked the IR detector under the nose and carried no external pylons, except the centerline pylon.

MiG-23MLs begun to replace the earlier MiG-23M in Soviet Regiments during the early 1980s. By the mid-1980s, most frontline regiments in the Soviet Union and Soviet regiments based in WARSAW Pact countries were re-equipped with Flogger Gs. As they were replaced, the MiG-23M Flogger Bs were either exported, used as trainers or held in reserve.

While most MiG-23Ms had been delivered in an overall air superiority Gray camouflage, most MiG-23ML Flogger Gs are delivered from the factory in a tactical camouflage scheme. The undersurfaces are painted in a Sky Blue, while the uppersurfaces are painted in three standard colors, although there is no standard pattern. Soviet requirements for camouflage simply state that "the upper surfaces should be effectively camouflaged." The colors used on most Soviet fighters are Dark and Light Olive Green, Light Brown and Earth Brown, although colors may vary on exported aircraft.

The Democratic Peoples Republic of Korea was the first non-WARSAW Pact coun-try to receive the Flogger G. Eight aircraft were delivered during September of 1984 and, on 8 May 1985, two were lost in a mid-air collision. Additional aircraft have been delivered and it is believed that North Korea operates a force of some forty-six Flogger Gs. Reportedly, these aircraft were given to Korea in order to obtain overflight rights for Soviet aircraft including Tu 16 Badgers, Tu 95 Bear C and Bear D reconnaissance aircraft engaged in maritime surveillance operations.

Currently, two WARSAW Pact countries are known to operate the MiG-23ML Flogger G, the German Democratic Republic and Czechoslovakia, both receiving their first Flogger Gs during 1985. Several mixed regiments (i.e. MiG-23s and MiG-21s within the same regiment) of the 7th Air Defense Army in Czechoslovakia operate flights of fifteen aircraft each equipped with both MiG-23MFs and MLs. It is believed that there are at least forty-five Flogger Gs in the Czech inventory.

The East German *Jagdfliegergeschwader 9 Heinrich Rau* at Peenemunde is currently in the process of replacing their Flogger Bs with Flogger Gs. The East Germans camouflage their aircraft with different colors than are used on Soviet Floggers. The forward portion of the fuselage undersurfaces and wing undersurfaces are in Sky Blue, while the rear portion of the fuselage undersurface is painted in Light Gray (it must be noted that a number of MiG-23 Flogger B/E/Gs have been observed painted Light Gray on all undersurfaces). The uppersurfaces are usually painted in a Brown and Green camouflage pattern, although the two primary colors can vary in shade. Known colors used on East German Floggers are Light Green, Dark Green, and Sand Brown. Three digit Red tactical numbers are used denoting the aircraft as belonging to a combat unit. On some occasions the first digit of the tactical is overpainted or a "1" is painted at the end of the number as a security measure to confuse Western intelligence agencies.

A MiG-23ML of *Jagdfliegergeschwader 9 Heinrich Rau* on the taxiway at Holzdorf Air Base. The first digit of the aircraft's true tactical number, Red 569, has been over painted for security reasons. The Winged Q symbol on the nose is an award for excellent maintenance and the Yellow star in the Q stands for a second award.

While personal markings or squadron badges are rarely seen on Floggers, it is quite common to see the *Otlitshnij Samoliot* badge on nose. This badge is a maintenance award carried on aircraft which fly a required number of hours trouble free and are in good overall condition. This award must be recertified every three months and if the aircraft fails an inspection the badge is removed. A similar award is given by the East German Air Force, known as the *Flugzeug der ausgezeichneten Qualität*. The badge is carried on the nose in the form of a winged "Q". The method of receiving the award is the same as in the Soviet Air Force; however, if the aircraft passes its next inspection a Yellow star is added (maximum three stars).

Nose Development

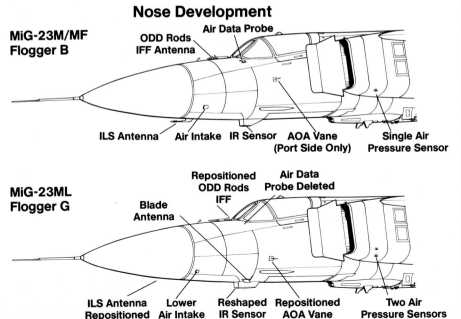

MiG-23M/MF Flogger B

ODD Rods
IFF Antenna
Air Data Probe
ILS Antenna   Air Intake   IR Sensor   AOA Vane (Port Side Only)   Single Air Pressure Sensor

MiG-23ML Flogger G

Blade Antenna
Repositioned ODD Rods IFF
Air Data Probe Deleted
ILS Antenna Repositioned To Starboard   Lower Air Intake   Reshaped IR Sensor   Repositioned AOA Vane (Both Sides)   Two Air Pressure Sensors

A pair of East German Air Force MiG-23ML Flogger Gs over the German coast near their base at Peenemünde. Both aircraft have had their tactical numbers altered for security reasons and each carries an extra 1 behind the true tactical number. The aircraft in the foreground is Red 551 and the Flogger in background is Red 610.

Red 610, A MiG-23ML Flogger G of the East German Air Force on the taxiway at Peenemünde Air Base, East Germany. A slightly lighter Red 1 has been added in front of the true tactical number (610) on the nose. The aircraft is carrying a R-60 (AA-8) missile rail on the fuselage pylon.

An East German Air Force MiG-23ML takes off from Holzdorf Air Base armed with four R-60 (AA-8) Aphid air-to-air missiles carried on dual launcher rails on the fuselage pylons. This Flogger is home based at Peenemünde Air Base, home of JFG 9.

Red 569, an East German Air Force MiG-23ML Flogger G, on the taxiway at Holzdorf Air Base on 29 August 1985. Although primarily an interceptor/fighter, the Flogger G can also be used for ground attack missions. This Flogger G carries a four pack multiple ejector bomb rack on each wing glove pylon for a total of eight FAB 100 bombs.

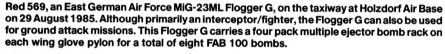

Rear Fuselage Development

MiG-23M/MF Flogger B

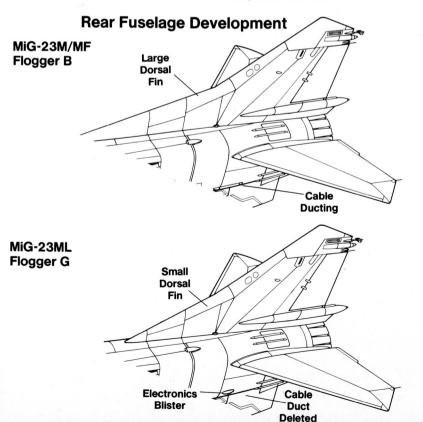

Large Dorsal Fin

Cable Ducting

MiG-23ML Flogger G

Small Dorsal Fin

Electronics Blister

Cable Duct Deleted

22

A pair of MiG-23ML Flogger Gs taxi out for a training sortie. Red 01 is carrying single R-60 (AA-8) Aphid missile rails on the fuselage pylons, R-23 (AA-7) Apex rails on the wing pylons and a fuel tank on the centerline pylon.

Blue 04, a MiG-23ML Flogger G of a Soviet Air Defense Regiment. The aircraft carries a four color uppersurface tactical camouflage consisting of two shades of Green and two of Brown over Light Blue undersurfaces (the rear portion of the fuselage is in Light Gray)

Yellow 30, a MiG-23ML Flogger G, carries a Soviet Guards Regiment insignia on the nose in front of the aircraft's tactical number. The Flogger in the foreground is equipped with AA-8 Aphid dual missile launch rails on the fuselage pylons.

MiG-23ML Flogger Gs of an unidentified Soviet fighter regiment on the snowy ramp of a Soviet air base. The wire attached to the underside of the nose of each aircraft is a communications line used by the ground crews to talk to the pilots.

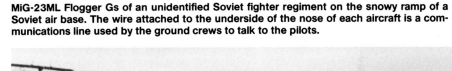

23

A Soviet pilot runs to his MiG-23ML Flogger G, White 60. The Flogger is armed with an AA-7 Apex radar guided missile on the wing glove pylon and an AA-8 Aphid IR guided missile on the fuselage pylon. It is interesting that, while the fuselage pylon has a dual launcher rail on it, only one AA-8 is carried.

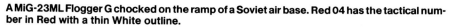

A MiG-23ML Flogger G chocked on the ramp of a Soviet air base. Red 04 has the tactical number in Red with a thin White outline.

East German ground crewmen prepare Red 339, MiG-23ML Flogger G for a mission. The man on the wing has removed the canvas canopy cover and the crewman on the ground is removing the blow-in door cover. The air intake covers are Red with the aircraft number painted on them in Black.

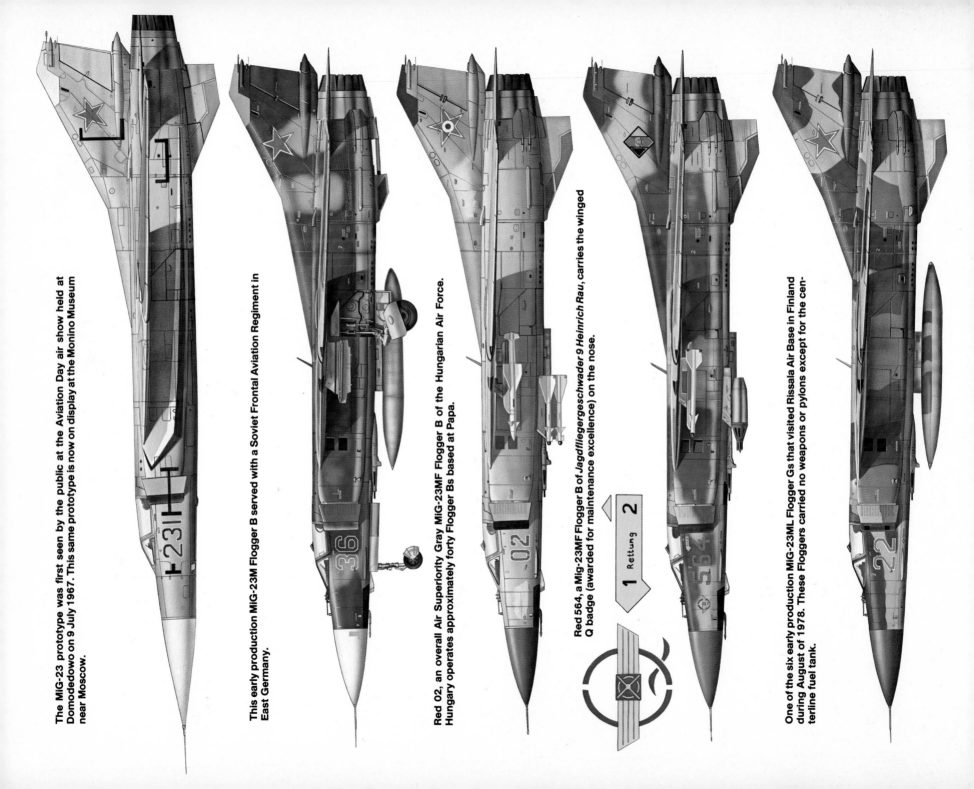

The MiG-23 prototype was first seen by the public at the Aviation Day air show held at Domodedowo on 9 July 1967. This same prototype is now on display at the Monino Museum near Moscow.

This early production MiG-23M Flogger B served with a Soviet Frontal Aviation Regiment in East Germany.

Red 02, an overall Air Superiority Gray MiG-23MF Flogger B of the Hungarian Air Force. Hungary operates approximately forty Flogger Bs based at Papa.

Red 564, a Mig-23MF Flogger B of *Jagdfliegergeschwader 9 Heinrich Rau*, carries the winged Q badge (awarded for maintenance excellence) on the nose.

Rettung
1   2

One of the six early production MiG-23ML Flogger Gs that visited Rissala Air Base in Finland during August of 1978. These Floggers carried no weapons or pylons except for the centerline fuel tank.

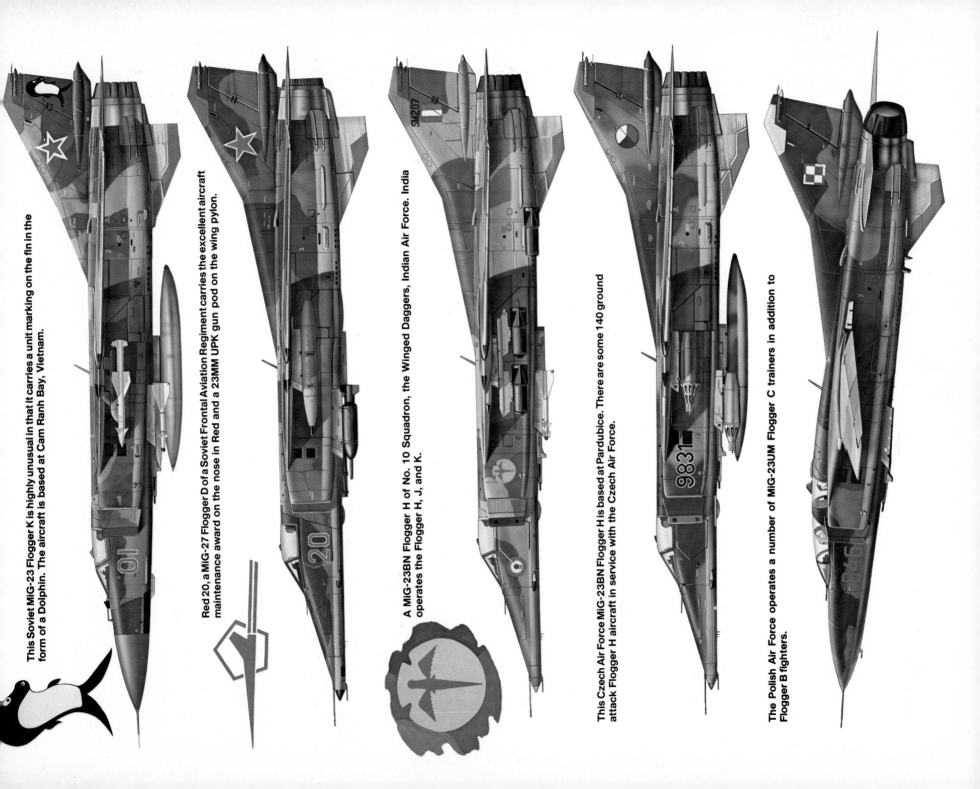

This Soviet MiG-23 Flogger K is highly unusual in that it carries a unit marking on the fin in the form of a Dolphin. The aircraft is based at Cam Ranh Bay, Vietnam.

Red 20, a MiG-27 Flogger D of a Soviet Frontal Aviation Regiment carries the excellent aircraft maintenance award on the nose in Red and a 23MM UPK gun pod on the wing pylon.

A MiG-23BN Flogger H of No. 10 Squadron, the Winged Daggers, Indian Air Force. India operates the Flogger H, J, and K.

This Czech Air Force MiG-23BN Flogger H is based at Pardubice. There are some 140 ground attack Flogger H aircraft in service with the Czech Air Force.

The Polish Air Force operates a number of MiG-23UM Flogger C trainers in addition to Flogger B fighters.

Floggers in Afghanistan

During August of 1986, the Soviets deployed a regiment of forty-five MiG-23ML Flogger Gs to Afghanistan. These aircraft were soon in combat flying initially from Kabul and later from Bagram Air Base. While the MiG-23ML Flogger G is primarily an air-to-air fighter/interceptor, the Flogger Gs deployed to Afghanistan were used almost exclusively in the air-to-ground role. It is believed that this deployment was undertaken as an operational test and evaluation to determine the capabilities of the Flogger G in its secondary role of ground attack under actual combat conditions.

The Floggers deployed to Afghanistan soon began to carry some unusual markings. To mark successful bombing missions, a number of the aircraft were painted with White stars under the cockpit. Each star represented one sortie and these missions markings represented the total flown by a particular aircraft, not necessarily the pilot that flew it.

One of the Squadron Commanders of the Flogger regiment was MAJ Anatolij Stiepaniuk who usually flew a Flogger G with the tactical number White 38 and twenty-seven mission stars under the cockpit. Another well known pilot was COL Anatolij Levchenko, who flew a total of 188 combat missions, 174 of which were ground attack sorties. COL Levchenko flew his last mission on 27 December 1986. This mission was his third of the day and was a bombing mission against Mudjahedin anti-aircraft artillery positions along the Salang road. His formation of Floggers would hit the enemy anti-aircraft positions near the city of Charikara on the Salang Pass road, while other aircraft supplied close air support to Soviet ground forces in the area.

Just after his flight of four Flogger Gs dropped their bomb loads on the enemy target, the COL's aircraft was hit by cannon fire in the starboard wing and set on fire. Knowing that his aircraft was fatally crippled and would soon go out of control, COL Levchenko dove the Flogger into the enemy anti-aircraft positions. He did not eject and for his actions on this mission, COL Levchenko was presented with one of the Soviet Union's highest awards, Hero of the Soviet Union.

Flogger Gs in Afghanistan carried chaff/flare launchers mounted on the upper fuselage. These were used to decoy IR guided, shoulder launched anti-aircraft missiles, such as the U.S. Stinger, fired by rebel forces.

(Above) MAJ Anatolij Stiepaniuk mans his MiG-23ML Flogger G, White 38, in Afghanistan. MAJ Stiepaniuk was a Ukranian pilot and the unit deputy commander for political affairs. The aircraft is highly unusual for a Soviet Air Force aircraft in that it is carrying mission markings in the form of White stars on the nose. These markings were for missions flown by the aircraft, not the pilot. (Wojciech Luczak)

(Below) A line-up of MiG-23ML Flogger Gs of a Soviet fighter regiment at Bagram Air Base, Afghanistan. White 38 carries a chaff/flare launcher mounted on the fuselage, used to decoy ground launched IR missiles. (Wojciech Luczak)

27

MiG-23 FLOGGER K

The latest fighter variant of the Flogger was first revealed to the West during 1986 when a US Navy F-4 Phantom crew observed a Flogger off the Vietnamese coast which featured a number of changes over earlier Flogger fighters. This sighting led NATO to assign this new Flogger variant the reporting name Flogger K. At this time, the Soviet designation for the Flogger K is unknown. While a number of earlier publications have identified this variant as either the MiG-23ML or MiG-23bis, both of these designations are now known to be incorrect.

The Flogger K differs from all earlier Flogger variants by having swiveling stores pylons mounted under the outer wing panels. Prior to the Flogger K, the only outer wing pylons used on the Flogger had been fixed pylons. Fuel tanks were normally carried on these pylons and in the event of combat, the tanks had to be jettisoned before the wing could be fully swept back. The new swiveling pylons are similar in function to those used on the General Dynamics F-111 and Panavia Tornado. It is known that the pylon can carry drop tanks and it is believed that it is wired to carry R-23 or later air-to-air missiles.

Another feature of the Flogger K was the introduction of a dogtooth notch in the inboard leading edge of the wing glove. This dogtooth notch generates vortices over the rear fuselage area which improve the aircraft's stability in yaw at high angles of attack and compensates for the loss of side area caused by the reduction of the dorsal fin area.

The standard three pole Odd Rods IFF antenna, which was used on all earlier variants of the Flogger (as well as many other Soviet tactical aircraft) was replaced by a blade style IFF antenna from 1986 onwards. Internally the MiG-23 Flogger K carries improved avionics including a lighter version of the High Lark radar. Most late production MiG-23 Flogger Ks have had the spray/debris guard removed from the nose wheel.

Other improvements have come in armament. In addition to the same variety of air-to-air weapons available to earlier variants, the Flogger K can carry newer air-to-air missiles such as the AA-11 Archer short range AAM and AA-10 Alamo (successor to the R-23 AA-7 Apex).

To date, no Flogger Ks have been exported outside the Soviet Union. A number of Soviet Air Force Flogger Ks were deployed to the German Democratic Republic as part of the Group of Soviet Forces in Germany. During 1984, the Soviet Union deployed a squadron of fourteen MiG-23 Flogger Ks to Cam Ranh Bay in Vietnam. These aircraft were deployed to provide air defense coverage for the large naval/air base being used by an increasingly large number of Soviet aircraft and ships. Additionally, these fighters were tasked to provide escort services for the Tu 16 Badgers and Tu 95 Bears which were also stationed at Cam Ranh Bay. During late 1989, the Soviets began to scale back this force and currently it is believed that there are only ten Tu 16s and MiG-23s remaining at the base. One interesting highlight concerning the Floggers stationed at Cam Ranh Bay is the fact that they are the only Soviet Flogger unit to be identified with a unit marking. These aircraft carry a Black and White figure of a standing Dolphin on the rudder.

In the Far East, a number of MiG-23 Flogger Ks were deployed to Etorofu Island. These islands are part of the Japanese Northern Territories which were occupied by the Red Army during the closing days of the Second World War. These islands are regarded by the Japanese to be part of their homeland and therefore illegally occupied. The Soviet Union has historically maintained a strong force on the island and has refused all efforts aimed at negotiating its return to Japan.

This MiG-23 Flogger K, Red 01, was based at Cam Ranh Bay, Vietnam, during 1988. The aircraft carries two AA-7 Apex, two AA-8 Aphid and a natural metal centerline fuel tank. This Flogger is highly unusual, in that it carries a unit marking on the rudder.

Forward Fuselage

MiG-23ML Flogger G

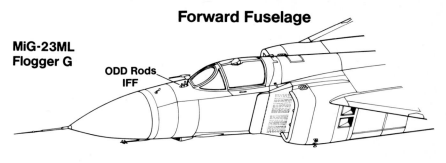

ODD Rods IFF

MiG-23 Flogger K

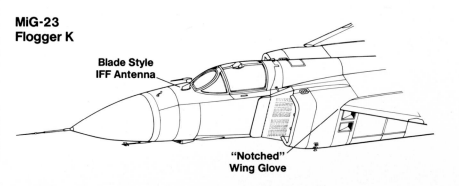

Blade Style IFF Antenna

"Notched" Wing Glove

This MiG-23 Flogger K carries fuel tanks on the centerline pylon and drop tanks on the wing station, outboard of the AA-7 Apex missiles. The Flogger K was the first Flogger variant equipped with outboard wing pylons that could swivel as the wing moved.

The MiG-23 Flogger K featured a modified notched wing glove and blade style IFF antennas replacing the earlier three pole Odd Rods IFF antennas. Red 34 has the wing swept forward and is at a high angle of attack as it tries to maintain formation with a U.S. Navy patrol aircraft during February of 1986.

Air-To-Air Weapons

R-23 (AA-7) Apex
(Flogger B, G, K)

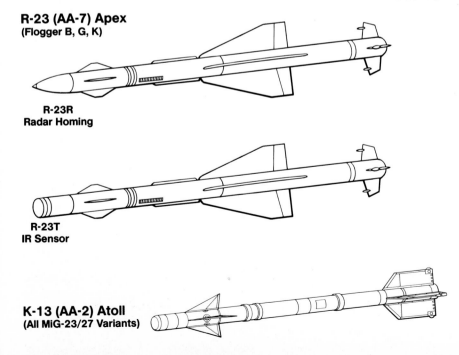

R-23R
Radar Homing

R-23T
IR Sensor

K-13 (AA-2) Atoll
(All MiG-23/27 Variants)

AA-10 Alamo
(Flogger K)

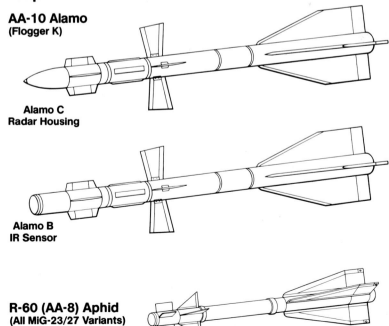

Alamo C
Radar Housing

Alamo B
IR Sensor

R-60 (AA-8) Aphid
(All MiG-23/27 Variants)

MiG-27 FLOGGER D

During the early 1970s the MiG OKB began work on a dedicated ground attack variant of the MiG-23MS fighter. To speed development, the airframe, wing, engine, and landing gear of the MiG-23 was retained for use in the attack variant. The swing wing would allow the aircraft to use short runways while carrying a heavy weapons load. The combination of small size, a more efficient swing wing, greater power, less fuel consumption and greater weapons loads than the Su-17 (just entering service) greatly impressed Soviet defense authorities and the MiG OKB was ordered to build a prototype of their proposed ground attack aircraft under the designation MiG-27.

The MiG OKB, under the leadership of Rostislav Belyakov, set about producing a prototype ground attack fighter which, although based on the MiG-23MS Flogger E, would be better suited to the new mission. A ground attack aircraft requires good all around visibility, while a high altitude capability and supersonic top speed are not as important as with an interceptor.

To improve the pilot's visibility forward and downward, the nose was completely redesigned becoming much shorter and wedge shaped. The new nose sloped sharply down from the cockpit to a pointed tip. To further improve pilot visibility, the canopy was redesigned with greater depth and the upper longitudinal frame (common on the MiG-23 fighter variants) was deleted. The wind screen assembly was made much deeper and sloped downward at a sharper angle than the wind screen of the fighter variants. In addition, it was restressed to withstand a bird strike and small arms fire. Because of the appearance of the new nose section, the MiG-27 quickly earned the nickname *Utkanos* (Duck nose).

The High Lark radar found in the interceptor variants was replaced by a laser range finder and marked target seeker mounted in the extreme forward portion of the nose. A terrain avoidance radar and a Type NI-50BM Doppler navigation radar are also carried in the nose along with a Type RV-3 (or RV-5) radio altimeter. Unlike the interceptor/fighter variants, the MiG-27 carries the Type SP-50 ILS antenna on the centerline of the nose below the glass viewing port of the laser range finder.

While the MiG-23 fighter carries a single Doppler radar blister on the port side of the fuselage in front of the nose wheel door, the MiG-27 is equipped with laterally mounted antennas on both the port and starboard side of the nose as well as a ventral Doppler antenna on the underside of the nose.

The Odd Rods IFF antenna and the yaw vanes are carried below the nose and the two air data probes for the intake control system are now carried on the upper nose near the port side of the canopy. Two large external armor plates have been added to either side of the fuselage under the cockpit to protect the pilot from small arms fire.

The nose wheel was strengthened and larger low pressure tires have been fitted to allow the aircraft to operate from forward airfields. To allow the extra space needed for the new tires in the wheel well, the nose wheel doors were bulged. The air data probe mast was located on the starboard side of the nose.

Since a ground attack aircraft is intended to operate at lower altitude than an interceptor, the engine installation on the MiG-27 was redesigned to give the aircraft better performance at low levels. The air intake splitter plates were made much smaller and are simpler than those found on the MiG-23 interceptor. These intakes are fixed and are not the variable geometry boundary layer type found on the MiG-23M Flogger B. The air intake itself is also slightly larger and somewhat bulged when viewed from the front.

The Tumansky R-29B used in the interceptor variants was replaced by a R-29-300 turbojet engine with a simpler afterburner and nozzle. This engine has a slightly reduced thrust rating in full afterburner; however, its dry thrust ratings is almost unchanged from the R-29B. By use of this simpler engine/nozzle configuration, both the installed engine weight and fuel consumption in subsonic cruise were drastically reduced.

The fuselage weapons pylons found on the MiG-23 fighter were replaced by weapons pylons fitted under the air intake ducts to allow the aircraft to carry larger diameter stores. Additionally, two rear fuselage weapons pylons were added, mounted on the fuselage sides behind the main landing gear wells. These pylons are stressed for weights up to at least 1,000 pounds. The GSh-23L cannon carried on the fuselage centerline of the fighter variants was replaced by a 30MM GSh-6-N-30 Gatling type six barrel cannon. This gun was installed in front of the fuselage centerline pylon and is almost entirely external. While this type of mounting has a high cost in increased drag, it eliminates the problem of possible explosions caused by a gun gas build-up, which had been experienced with internally mounted weapons. The gun is fed with rounds carried in an ammunition box stored internally in the fuselage and it is believed that the magazine has a capacity of at least seven hundred rounds.

A missile control data link antenna was fitted to the starboard wing leading edge above the wing pylon and a TV camera was mounted above the weapons pylon on the port wing. The missile control antenna is associated with air-to-surface missiles such as the AS-7 Kerry and AS-9 anti-radiation missiles.

Apart from the shorter engine afterburner nozzle, the tail was virtually identical with that of the MiG-23MS Flogger E with the exception of the small air intake on the starboard side of the vertical stabilizer, which was deleted. Early production MiG-27s lacked trim tabs on the horizontal stabilizers; however, these were fitted on late production aircraft.

The MiG-27 prototype flew for the first time during 1972 and after successfully completing its evaluation trials, the type was put into production. A number of early production aircraft were deployed to the Group of Soviet Forces in Germany, where the aircraft was first spotted by the West. NATO gave the new ground attack variant the reporting name Flogger D. The GSFG operates three Flogger D regiments (with a strength of thirty aircraft each) based at Mirow, Altenburg and Finsterwalde in East Germany.

In October of 1988, the Soviet Union deployed approximately thirty MiG-27 Flogger Ds to Afghanistan for offensive operations against Afghan freedom fighters. These aircraft were based at Shindand AFB in the western part of Afghanistan and flew their first combat mission on 31 October, attacking guerrilla positions south of Kandahar, the country's second largest city. The MiG-27s remained in combat until 15 February 1989, when all Soviet forces withdrew from Afghanistan.

This Flogger D, Yellow 47, carries a short rail under the wing pylon intended for use with the 240MM S-240 unguided air-to-ground rocket, one of the largest unguided weapons in use by any air force.

There were very little external changes on the MiG-27 Flogger D during its production run; however, recently the Soviets have begun to remove the missile control radar antenna and TV camera pods from the wing glove leading edges and the debris guard from the nose wheel.

The MiG-27 Flogger D has seen widespread service with the Soviet Air Force and still equips a considerable number of frontline regiments. The MiG-27 Flogger D, however, was never exported outside the Soviet Union.

Fuselage Development

MiG-23M Flogger B

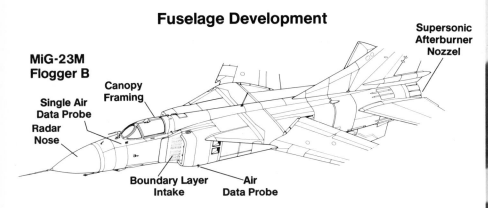

- Single Air Data Probe
- Radar Nose
- Canopy Framing
- Boundary Layer Intake
- Air Data Probe
- Supersonic Afterburner Nozzel

MiG-27 Flogger D

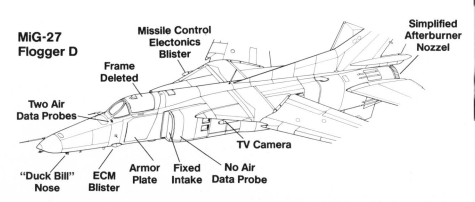

- Two Air Data Probes
- "Duck Bill" Nose
- ECM Blister
- Armor Plate
- Fixed Intake
- No Air Data Probe
- Frame Deleted
- Missile Control Electonics Blister
- TV Camera
- Simplified Afterburner Nozzel

A Soviet Air Force pilot mans his MiG-27 Flogger D. The dark panel under the nose is the dielectric panel for the Doppler navigation radar, while the smaller dark panel just in front of the nose wheel well is the dielctric panel for the radar altimeter.

31

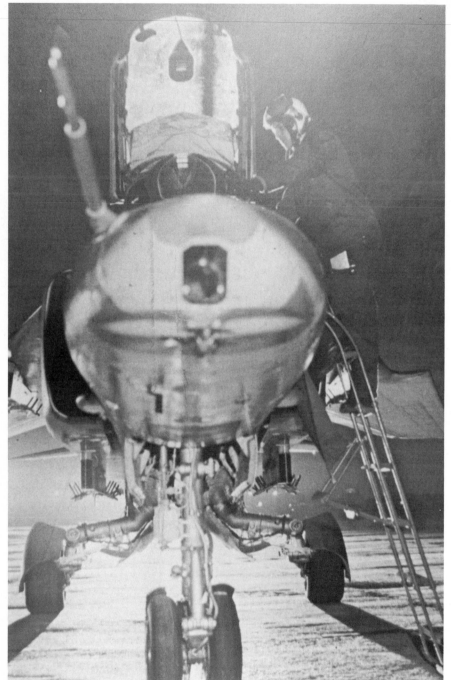

Four MiG-27 Flogger Ds of a Frontal Aviation squadron commanded by MAJ I. Ivanov are parked on a taxiway during Exercise Sever, a Soviet tactical exercise held during 1979. The lead aircraft's tactical number, Yellow 44, is painted on the exterior armor plating.

A Soviet pilot mans his MiG-27 Flogger D for a winter mission. Besides the center rear view mirror housing in the top of the canopy, this Flogger is also equipped with two additional mirrors on the canopy framing. The clear panel in the nose is the view port for the laser range finder.

Fuselage Development

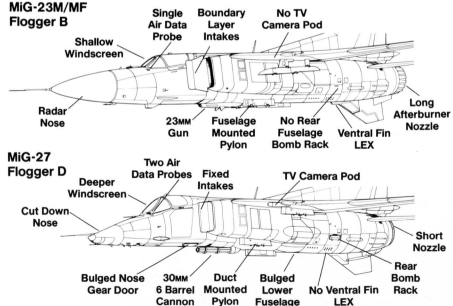

MiG-23M/MF Flogger B

Shallow Windscreen

Single Air Data Probe

Boundary Layer Intakes

No TV Camera Pod

Radar Nose

23mm Gun

Fuselage Mounted Pylon

No Rear Fuselage Bomb Rack

Ventral Fin LEX

Long Afterburner Nozzle

MiG-27 Flogger D

Deeper Windscreen

Two Air Data Probes

Fixed Intakes

TV Camera Pod

Cut Down Nose

Bulged Nose Gear Door

30mm 6 Barrel Cannon

Duct Mounted Pylon

Bulged Lower Fuselage

No Ventral Fin LEX

Rear Bomb Rack

Short Nozzle

This Soviet Frontal Aviation MiG-27 Flogger D, Red 20, carries the *Otlitshnij Samoljot* maintenance excellence badge on the nose in front of the tactical number.

This pair of MiG-27 Flogger Ds are being used in their alternate role of air defense and are armed with K-13 (AA-2) Atoll air-to-air missiles on the wing pylons.

A pair of MiG-27 Flogger Ds on the runway prior to takeoff. The Flogger D has a simplified air intake duct which is far different than the fighter MiG-23s. The GSh-23L 23MM cannon common on the fighter variants is replaced by a six-barrel GSh-6-N30 30MM Gatling type cannon.

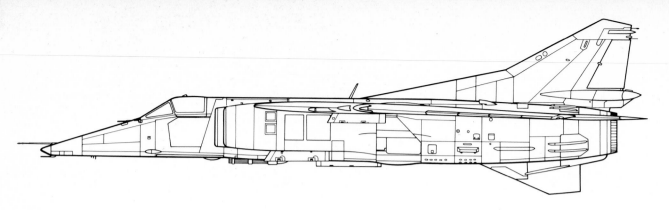

Specifications

MiG-27 Flogger D

Wingspan .46 feet 9 inches
Length . . . . .52 feet 6 inches
Height . . . . .18 feet ½ inch
Empty Weight . . . . .18,075 pounds
Maximum Weight . . . . .44,313 pounds
Powerplant . . . . .One 25,350 lbst Tumanksy R-29-300
                               turbojet engine

Armament .One GSh-6-N-30 30 ММ cannon and
                               up to 9,920 pounds of ordnance.

Performance
   Maximum Speed . . . . .1,275 mph (Mach 1.7)
   Service ceiling . . . . .52,500 feet
   Range .1,550 miles (three tanks)
Crew . . . . .One

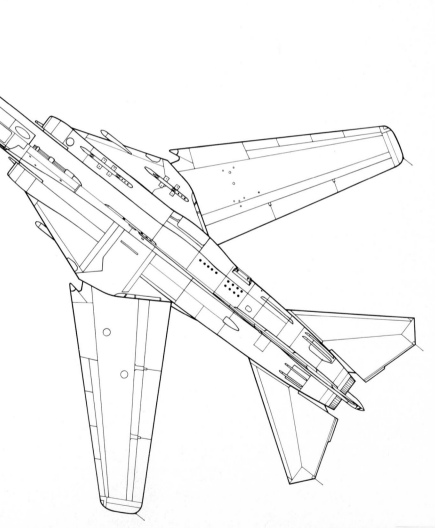

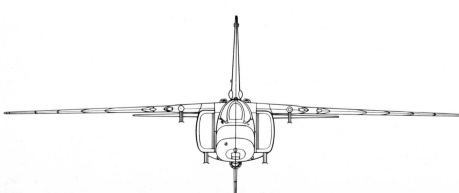

This late production MiG-27 Flogger D has the bullet wing fairings deleted and carries the new twenty shot 80MM rocket pods on the wing pylon. This pod is currently replacing the earlier UB-l6/32 57MM rocket pods as the standard Soviet air-to-ground rocket armament.

A MiG-27 Flogger D of a Soviet Frontal Aviation Regiment is towed along a taxiway on an air base in East Germany. The Flogger regiment is attached to the Group of Soviet Forces, Germany (GSFG).

A MiG-27 Flogger D being towed out of its shelter on a forward airfield. This is an early production Flogger D and lacks the trim tabs on the horizontal stabilizers that were fitted to late production aircraft. This Flogger D is armed with two UB-32 rocket pods on the wing pylons.

This late production MiG-27 Flogger D carries a R-60 (AA-8) Aphid missile launcher rail on the wing glove pylon. The missile control antenna pod, normally carried on the wing glove leading edge was deleted on late production MiG-27 Flogger Ds.

MiG-23B/BN FLOGGER F/H

The Soviets developed a second ground attack variant of the MiG-23 in an effort to simplify the procurement of spare parts and to produce an export variant that would be compatible with the interceptor/fighter variants already offered for export. This aircraft had the nose section of the MiG-27 mated with the airframe of the MiG-23MS Flogger E.

Development of this hybrid ground attack aircraft began during the early 1970s and the first experimental prototype was flown during 1973. After a successful evaluation, the type entered production that same year. Aircraft built for service with the Soviet Air Force received the designation MiG-23B, while those built for export were designated as MiG-23BNs.

The MiG-23B/BN differs from the MiG-27 in a number of ways. The most obvious difference is in the engine air intakes. The MiG-23BN is equipped with the variable geometry boundary layer intakes used on the fighter variants of the MiG-23, although the pressure sensors found on the intakes of fighter variants have been relocated to the port side of the cockpit canopy.

To afford a larger degree of compatibility with the fighter variants, the six barrel 30MM GSh-6-N-30 cannon was replaced with the GSh-23L twin barrel 23MM cannon.

The MiG-23BN uses the same Tumansky R-29-300 powerplant as the MiG-27 Flogger D along with the short afterburner nozzle. With the variable geometry air intakes, the MiG-23BN has a somewhat better performance than the MiG-27 at high speeds, giving the aircraft a secondary air defense capability. The lack of an air intercept radar, however, makes the MiG-23BN incapable of carrying beyond visual range radar guided air-to-air missiles, such as the R-23 (AA-7) Apex. MiG-23B/BNs can carry infrared missiles, such as the K-13 (AA-2) Atoll, R-60 (AA-8) Aphid, and AA-11 Archer.

The MiG-23B/BN has the missile control pod relocated from the wing leading edge to a position just in front of the starboard wing glove pylon. As with the MiG-27, the MiG-23B/BN has two bomb racks mounted on the rear fuselage to the rear of the main wheel wells. The MiG-23B/BN can carry the same weapons load and armament as the earlier Flogger D, although the weapons pylons are relocated from the air intake duct to the underside of the fuselage. Guided weapons include the AS-7 Kerry, AS-10 Karen and AS-14 Kedge air-to-surface missiles (when the AS-14 is carried, a laser guidance pod is normally fitted to the centerline pylon). A large variety of unguided weapons can be carried by the MiG-23B/BN including UB-16 and UB-32 rocket pods (16 or 32 shot 57MM S-5 unguided rockets) and various bombs. The rocket pods are beginning to be replaced by a large twenty shot pod containing 80MM unguided hollow charge rockets. Single S-240 rockets can also be carried.

Free fall weapons include FAB 100 and FAB 500 bombs, PTK 250 cluster dispensers, RPK-100 fragmentation bombs, BETA B-25 concrete piercing bombs and a 500 kg (1,102 pound) laser guided bomb. There are two different types of gun pods carried, a UPK-23 twin 23MM gun pod and a single barrel 23MM cannon pod in which the gun is depressed approximately 15 degrees for engaging ground targets.

Two different kinds of multiple bomb racks are currently in use; a twin bomb carrier/ejector rack for large weapons and a four bomb rack capable of carrying four FAB 100 or FAB 250 bombs. This rack is similar in design to the six bomb multiple bomb rack used on the Su-17M-4 Fitter K. The four bomb rack can be carried on all four weapons pylons and with two additional bombs being carried on the rear fuselage racks, the MiG-23B/BN can deliver an impressive load of eighteen bombs. Both the fuselage centerline pylon and outboard wing pylons are capable of carrying several different size drop tanks.

The MiG-23B/BN can be configured for the tactical nuclear strike role with TN-1000 or TN-1200 tactical nuclear bombs. It is believed that the MiG-23B/BN can also carry the

A Czech Air Force MiG-23BN Flogger H, Black 9550, rolls out with both the wing flaps and slats fully extended. The braking parachute is also deployed from its housing at the base of the rudder.

A Czech pilot mans his MiG-23BN, Black 9831. This Flogger H is armed with UB-16 rocket pods on the fuselage pylons and UB-32 rocket pods on the wing pylons. The helmets on the boarding ladder belong to the ground crew and provide both hearing protection and communications.

Fuel/Air Explosive (FAE) weapon, which resembles a large drop tank and was used in Afghanistan with devastating effects. FAE weapons are used primarily to attack large area targets such as troop concentrations, airfields and villages. The weapon has a lethal radius of up to 1,300 feet and produces a huge fire ball. FAE weapons kill by fire, burning off the oxygen in the air, and from the tremendous over-pressure caused by the blast.

The MiG-23B serves in large numbers with Soviet Frontal Aviation Regiments, while the export MiG-23BN has seen considerable export success. The first export aircraft were supplied to Middle Eastern nations. Egypt received a number of MiG-23BNs, basing them at Mersa Matruh. As the political climate between the Soviet Union and Egypt changed and the Soviets cut off spare parts for the Floggers, the aircraft were put in storage. Reportedly, most were later sold to the USAF, while several others were passed to China. Other Middle East operators of the MiG-23BN are Algeria, Libya, Syria and Iraq.

When these exported MiG-23BNs were first observed by the West, NATO assigned the aircraft the reporting name Flogger F. It is not known if NATO intelligence specialist missed the lateral antennas mounted on the port and starboard sides of the fuselage above the nose wheel door, or if they were not carried on early MiG-23BNs. When these antennas were detected, NATO assigned aircraft with the antennas the reporting name Flogger H, to distinguish these MiG-23BNs from those without the antennas (it is believed that there were, in fact, no MiG-23BNs produced without the lateral antennas.)

Besides the Middle East, MiG-23BNs are flown by Cuba, Ethiopia, Angola and recently there have been reports that Sudan has received an unspecified number of Floggers from an unidentified source.

India operates both the MiG-27 Flogger J and MiG-23BN Flogger H. The first aircraft received were MiG-23BNs, some delivered assembled directly from the Soviet Union, while other were received as knocked down kits. Assembly of these by Hindustan Aeronatics Ltd. at Nasik began during 1984 with the first operational MiG-23BN unit, No 10 Winged Dagger Squadron, being declared combat ready during 1985.

Three WARSAW Pact countries operate MiG-23BNs, Bulgaria, Czechoslovakia and East Germany. The first country to obtain the MiG-23BN was Czechoslovakia during 1979, followed by East Germany during 1981. Currently, the Czech Air Force has an inventory of some 140 Flogger Hs, organized into three flights based at Bechyne, Hradec Kralove and Pardubice Air Base (east of Prague), and another flight based at Namesti Nad Oslanow. This regiment is under the operational control of the 10th Tactical Air Army. The German Democratic Republic also operates some thirty MiG-23BNs assigned to *Jagdbombenfliegergeschwader 31 Klement Gottwald* at Drewitz. This unit has a reputation for a maintaining a particularly high standard of operational readiness with their Floggers. Bulgaria operates a regiment of thirty-six Flogger H aircraft. These aircraft carry two digit White tactical numbers and also have the national insignia on both the rear fuselage and vertical fin.

The MiG-23BN can carry a larger weapons load than its stablemate, the Sukhoi Su-17 Fitter K; however, losses to accidents are considerably higher in Flogger equipped units. The flight characteristics of the MiG-23BN are much more demanding than those of the Sukhoi and as a result the Fitter is more popular among Soviet and WARSAW Pact ground attack pilots than the Flogger H.

This Czech MiG-23BN, Black 9831, taxies out at Pardubice Air Base for another sortie. The Flogger is armed with natural metal UB-16 rocket pods on the fuselage pylons and UB-32 rocket pods on the wing pylons.

Czech ground crewmen work on the nose gear of MiG-23BN, Black 9142. The panel just in front of the nose wheel well is the radar altimeter and the two dielectric blisters on the fuselage sides above the wheel well are reportedly target laser illumination receivers for use with air-to-surface missiles. This aircraft has the starboard wing glove electronics pod removed.

The pilot of this MiG-23BN, Black 9142, on the flight line at Pardubice Air Base, is performing pre-flight checks with the debris guards in place on the fuselage blow in doors. The wire attached to the nose is for communications between the pilot and ground crew.

Fuselage Development

MiG-27 Flogger D

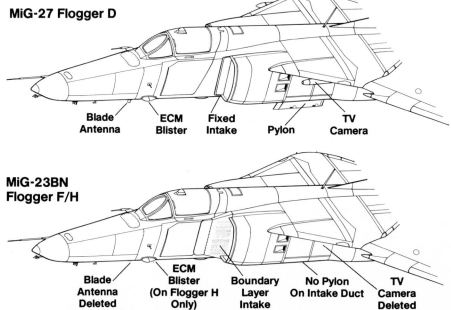

Blade Antenna   ECM Blister   Fixed Intake   Pylon   TV Camera

MiG-23BN Flogger F/H

Blade Antenna Deleted   ECM Blister (On Flogger H Only)   Boundary Layer Intake   No Pylon On Intake Duct   TV Camera Deleted

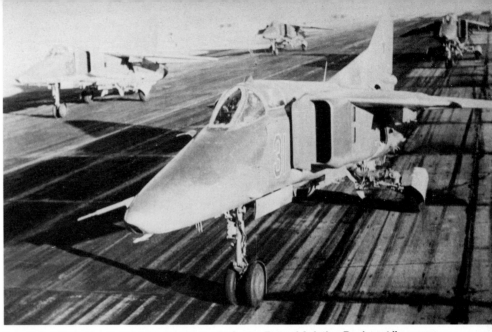

This Czech Air Force MiG-23BN Flogger H, Black 9550, has the tactical number outlined in White. This Flogger has an early style overall White braking parachute, rather than one of the more current style White and Red parachutes.

Four MiG-23BN Flogger H fighter-bombers of a Soviet Frontal Aviation Regiment line up on the runway for a section takeoff. The tactical number on Red 31 (foreground) has a White outline, while Red 53 (left) has no outline.

MiG-23BN Flogger H fighter-bombers of No 10 Winged Dagger Squadron, Indian Air Force on the flight line of their home base. India has both the MiG-23BN and MiG-27M in front line service and produces the MiG-27M under license.

A pair of East German Air Force MiG-23BNs of *Jagdbobenfliegergeschwader Klement Gottwald*, based at Drewitz. Both aircraft have had the first digit of the tactical number over painted. Aircraft 12 is actually Red 712 and aircraft 10 is Red 710.

A Czech MiG-23BN Flogger H takes off from Pardubice Air Base. With the wing full forward the Flogger has good short field performance. The ventral fin is nearly in the flight position, being slaved to the nose wheel, which is half retracted. The main landing gear has not yet started to retract.

Soviet ground crewmen load 23MM ammunition into the internal ammunition box of a MiG-23BN. The ammunition box is lowered for loading by a built-in winch (behind the man on the right). The bomb on the fuselage rack is a FAB 500 (500 kg/1,102 pound) bomb.

A Czech Air Force MiG-23BN Flogger H taxies out for another mission. The wings are normally kept in the fully swept back position while taxiing and will be swept fully forward just before takeoff. The aircraft in the background are MiG-23UM Flogger C trainers.

Lower Fuselage Development

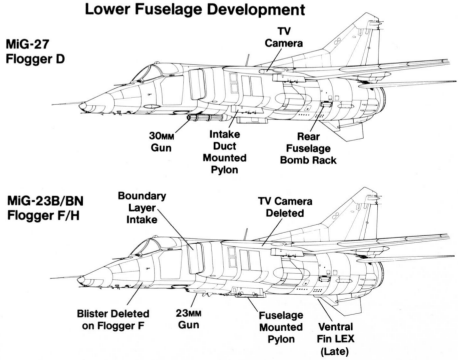

MiG-27 Flogger D

TV Camera

30MM Gun

Intake Duct Mounted Pylon

Rear Fuselage Bomb Rack

MiG-23B/BN Flogger F/H

Boundary Layer Intake

TV Camera Deleted

Blister Deleted on Flogger F

23MM Gun

Fuselage Mounted Pylon

Ventral Fin LEX (Late)

Czech Air Force MiG-23BN Flogger H fighter-bombers being serviced on the flight line of Pardubice Air Base on a rainy day. The second aircraft in the row, Black 5741, is being refueled by a Tatra fuel truck.

Red 715, a MiG-23BN Flogger H of the East German Air Force, taxies out at Holzdorf on 29 August 1985. The Flogger is armed with four pack bomb racks on the wing and fuselage pylons and a single FAB 100 bomb on the rear fuselage bomb rack for a total of eighteen 220 pound bombs.

Air-To-Ground Weapons

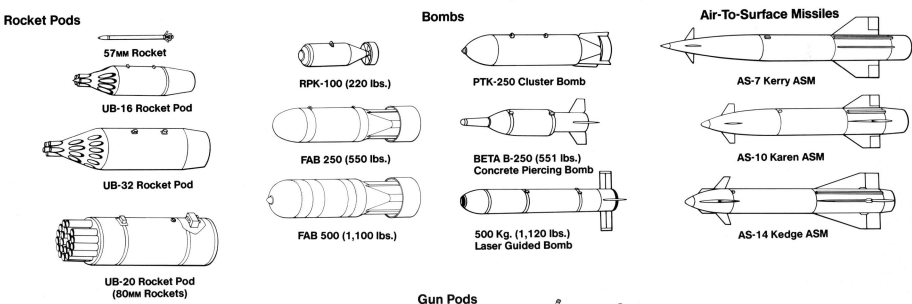

Rocket Pods

57ᴍᴍ Rocket

UB-16 Rocket Pod

UB-32 Rocket Pod

UB-20 Rocket Pod (80ᴍᴍ Rockets)

Bombs

RPK-100 (220 lbs.)

FAB 250 (550 lbs.)

FAB 500 (1,100 lbs.)

PTK-250 Cluster Bomb

BETA B-250 (551 lbs.) Concrete Piercing Bomb

500 Kg. (1,120 lbs.) Laser Guided Bomb

Air-To-Surface Missiles

AS-7 Kerry ASM

AS-10 Karen ASM

AS-14 Kedge ASM

Gun Pods

UPK-23 Twin Gun Pod

Single Barrel Depressed Angle 23ᴍᴍ Gun Pod

41

A Czech Air Force pilot mans his MiG-23BN Flogger H fighter-bomber at a Czech air base. The aircraft in the background is a MiG-21MF Fishbed J air superiority fighter, which is currently being phased out in favor of the MiG-29 Fulcrum.

The interior of the MiG-23BN cockpit is painted in a Blue-Green color with Black instrument faces and switches. There are a number of differences between the cockpit of the MiG-23 fighter and the fighter-bomber, particularly in the radar equipment installed and the gunsights.

This MiG-23BN, Black 9829, is being towed along the taxiway at Pardubice by an eight wheeled cargo truck. The Flogger is configured with missile rails for AA-8 Aphid air-to-air missiles on the wing pylons and has the ventral fin LEX which was first introduced on the MiG-23BN.

Multiple Bomb Racks

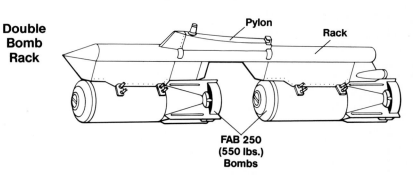

Double Bomb Rack

Pylon

Rack

FAB 250 (550 lbs.) Bombs

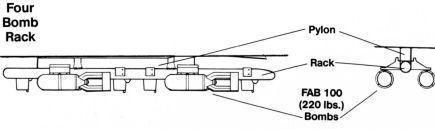

Four Bomb Rack

Pylon

Rack

FAB 100 (220 lbs.) Bombs

MiG-27M FLOGGER J

During the late 1960s, the MiG OKB developed an improved variant of the MiG-27 Flogger D under the designation MiG-27M. The basic Flogger D airframe was retained and the aircraft was outfitted with new and improved avionics.

The MiG-27M was first identified by NATO during 1981 and assigned the NATO reporting name Flogger J. The nose of the MiG-27M differed from the MiG-27 in a number of ways. A chin blister, housing a Laser Target Designator System (LTDS) was added to the nose, the ILS antenna was relocated from the centerline of the nose to the port side, the Odd Rods IFF antenna carried below the nose was replaced by a blade type IFF antenna and the single angle of attack transmitter carried on the port side of the MiG-27 was replaced by two angle of attack transmitters carried on both the port and starboard side of the nose.

The LTDS detects laser energy from an illuminated target and feeds range and bearing information directly into the onboard fire control computer. The computer then automatically releases the weapon selected by the pilot, firing weapons at the proper distance from the target to ensure a hit.

The MiG-27M also featured a change to the gun mounting. Small fins were added to each side of the lower fuselage in line with the gun muzzle to reduce gun gas ingestion by the engine. The rear portion of the gun itself was covered by a fairing to protect the gun operating gear from foreign object damage.

As with late production MiG-27 Flogger Ds, the missile control pod and television camera pod on the wing glove leading edges were deleted. The wing glove area was modified with the addition of a leading edge extension (LEX) to improve low speed/high angle of attack performance.

The Indian government selected the MiG-27 to meet its strike fighter/fighter-bomber requirement and obtained a license to produce the aircraft in India. Built by Hindustan Aeronautics Ltd. (HAL) at Nasik, India, the MiG-27 will replace the MiG-23BN Flogger H on HAL production lines (both the MiG-23BN and MiG-27M are known as the *Bahadur* Valiant in Indian Air Force service). The first MiG-27M, assembled from major subassemblies built in the Soviet Union, was completed on 11 January 1986. During the next phase of production HAL assembled aircraft from component kits provided by the Soviets. During 1988, HAL began fabrication of detail parts from raw materials and began total manufacture of the aircraft. The Tumansky R-29-300 powerplant is also built under license at the HAL plant at Koraput, while the aircraft's instruments are built by HAL's Avionics Division at Hyderabad. The Indians plan to build approximately 165 MiG-27Ms.

Red 17, a Soviet Air Force MiG-27M Flogger J, carries an unusual armament load, a single FAB 100 bomb on the rear fuselage rack and a UB-16 rocket pod carried on the port fuselage pylon. This aircraft also has the nose wheel spray/debris cover deleted.

The MiG-27M Flogger J features a modified wing glove with a leading edge extension (LEX) which is thought to house electronics equipment,. The aircraft also has two small blast deflectors installed alongside the gun muzzle to prevent gun gas from being ingested by the air intakes.

Forward Fuselage Development

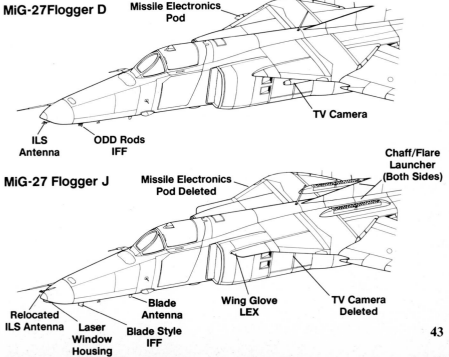

MiG-27 Flogger D

Missile Electronics Pod

TV Camera

ILS Antenna — ODD Rods IFF

MiG-27 Flogger J

Missile Electronics Pod Deleted

Chaff/Flare Launcher (Both Sides)

Relocated ILS Antenna — Laser Window Housing — Blade Antenna — Blade Style IFF — Wing Glove LEX — TV Camera Deleted

During the fighting in Afghanistan, the Soviets began outfitting their tactical aircraft with chaff/flare dispensers. This Flogger J has a dispenser mounted on top of the wing glove pylon; this mounting is also used on Flogger G fighters.

This MiG-27M Flogger J is carrying FAB 250 (550 pound) bombs on the front and rear fuselage/inlet duct pylons and rocket pods on the wing glove pylons. In addition, it has a chaff/flare dispenser on the top of the wing glove.

This MiG-27M Flogger J is equipped with dual missile launch rails on the wing pylons and single missile rails on the intake duct pylons for R-60 (AA-8) Aphid IR guided air-to-air missile. The aircraft's tactical number is 05.

Fuselage Development

MiG-27 Flogger D

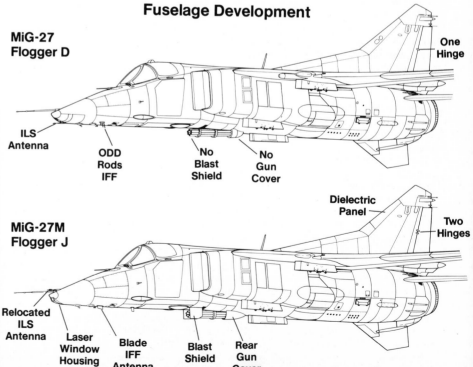

One Hinge

ILS Antenna

ODD Rods IFF

No Blast Shield

No Gun Cover

Dielectric Panel

Two Hinges

MiG-27M Flogger J

Relocated ILS Antenna

Laser Window Housing

Blade IFF Antenna

Blast Shield

Rear Gun Cover

MiG-23UM FLOGGER C

As is common Soviet practice, a two seat combat capable trainer variant of the MiG-23 was developed under the designation MiG-23UM. Based on the airframe of the MiG-23M/MS (Flogger E), the two aircraft were practically identical with the exception of the second cockpit. The MiG-23UM retains the overall length of the MiG-23M with the instructor's cockpit being installed in the fuselage behind the standard cockpit. The second cockpit is slightly raised to improve the instructor's forward vision, resulting in a heavier dorsal spine and a slightly humpbacked appearance.

Each cockpit has a separate canopy which is hinged to open upward. Neither canopy is fitted with the internal/external rear view mirrors found on the fighter variants of the Flogger. There are heavy oval glass windows fitted into the connecting framing between the two cockpits; however, these do nothing to improve the frontal view for the instructor. To give the instructor the necessary forward visibility for landings and takeoffs, a retractable periscope is mounted in the instructor's canopy which automatically deploys when the landing gear is lowered. A folding instrument flying hood is carried in the student's cockpit and when not in use, is stored behind the ejection seat.

Both cockpits are equipped with KM-1 zero-zero ejection seats and the seat in the students cockpit can be command ejected from the rear cockpit. The MiG-23UM control system features a cutout system that is activated whenever the instructor takes over control of the aircraft. The cutout automatically disconnects the student's controls as soon the instructor touches his control stick and/or rudder pedals.

Early production MiG-23UMs were powered by the Tumansky R-27-300 powerplant, although later production aircraft were powered by the R-29B. Externally, there is no differences between the early and late production aircraft.

The MiG-23UM is intended to train both fighter and attack pilots and as a result, the MiG-23UM carries an air-to-ground missile control antenna pod on the starboard wing glove pylon. The MiG-23UM is equipped with the Jay Bird air intercept radar (used on the Flogger E). The use of the small Jay Bird radar was dictated by the fact that the second cockpit was installed in the MiG-23UM by relocating avionics from the spine to the nose. To install the larger High Lark radar would have meant a reduction in internal fuel and a major redesign of the MiG-23UM's nose. This was felt to be unnecessary since students could be trained on the High Lark radar in a simulator and later in the single seat Flogger B/G/Ks. The MiG-23UM also lacks the infrared sensor carried under the nose on the fighter variants.

The MiG-23UM has a straight leading edge on the ventral fin without the leading edge extension. The rudder has a single hinge and early production MiG-23UMs lacked trim tabs on the horizontal stabilizers (which were added on later production aircraft).

For weapons training and combat exercises the MiG-23UM carries the underfuselage GSh-23L cannon, AA-2 Atoll and AA-8 Aphid air-to-air missiles. To train attack pilots, UB-16 or UB-32 rocket pods and/or bombs can be carried on the wing glove and fuselage pylons.

The first MiG-23UM was discovered by NATO shortly after the MiG-23MF Flogger B fighter and was assigned the NATO reporting name Flogger C. Most early Flogger Cs were delivered from the factory painted in an air superiority Gray camouflage, although later production aircraft were delivered in a multi-color tactical camouflage. Some Soviet Flogger Cs carry either Yellow or Orange tactical number; however, it is also common to outline the tactical number in White on aircraft carrying the tactical camouflage. Aircraft stationed inside the Soviet Union carry three digit tactical numbers which identify the aircraft as trainers assigned to a training unit.

The MiG-23UM has been exported to all countries which operate fighter and/or ground attack variants of the Flogger. Algeria, Afghanistan, Angola, Bulgaria, Cuba, Czechoslovakia, Egypt, Ethiopia, German Democratic Republic, Hungary, India, Iraq, North Korea, Libya, Poland, Rumania, and Syria all have Flogger Cs in their inventories.

It is uncommon for the Flogger C to be used in a combat role; however, on 28 October 1987 an Angolan Air Force Flogger C (flown by Cubans) was shot down by UNITA forces. The crew successfully ejected and was captured by UNITA rebels.

In WARSAW Pact countries, MiG-23UMs are assigned to both combat and advanced training units. In Czechoslovakia, Flogger Cs are assigned to all fighter and ground attack regiments, as well as the advanced training units at Prerov and Kosice. In Hungary, a small number of MiG-23UMs are assigned to the MiG-23MF regiment at Papa, while others serve with the training unit at Szolnok. While all Hungarian Flogger Bs are in air superiority Gray, the ex-Soviet Air Force Flogger Cs carry an air-to-ground tactical camouflage.

The East German Air Force has assigned their MiG-23UMs to *Jagdfliegergeschwader 9 Heinrich Rau* at Peenemunde, *Jagdbombenfliegergeschwader 31 Klement Gottwald* at Drewitz and *Jagdfliegerausbildungsgeschwader Leander Ratz* at Rothenburg. All East German MiG-23UMs carry Black three digit tactical numbers, denoting them as training aircraft (fighter and ground attack aircraft carry Red three digit tactical numbers).

A Soviet MiG-23UM Flogger C taxies out for a training mission on a Winter day. The tactical number consists of just a White outline, painted against the aircraft's camouflage finish.

This Soviet Air Force MiG-23UB Flogger C carries a tactical camouflage on the uppersurfaces. All Flogger Cs were delivered from the factory in air superiority Gray and were repainted during overhauls with the new camouflage.

An early production MiG-23UM Flogger C, Yellow 27, rolls out on the runway with the instructor's periscope deployed. Early MiG-23UMs were all painted in air superiority Gray, which has now been replaced by a tactical camouflage. An AA-2 Atoll missile rail is fitted to the wing pylon.

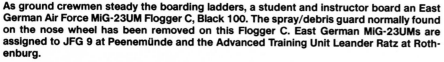

As ground crewmen steady the boarding ladders, a student and instructor board an East German Air Force MiG-23UM Flogger C, Black 100. The spray/debris guard normally found on the nose wheel has been removed on this Flogger C. East German MiG-23UMs are assigned to JFG 9 at Peenemünde and the Advanced Training Unit Leander Ratz at Rothenburg.

Fuselage Development

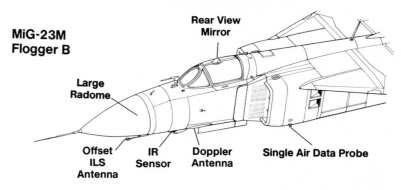

MiG-23M
Flogger B

Rear View Mirror

Large Radome

Offset ILS Antenna

IR Sensor

Doppler Antenna

Single Air Data Probe

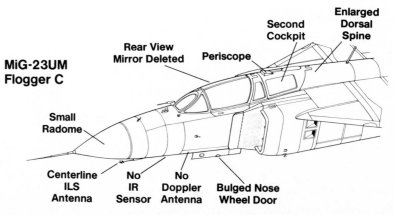

MiG-23UM
Flogger C

Rear View Mirror Deleted

Periscope

Second Cockpit

Enlarged Dorsal Spine

Small Radome

Centerline ILS Antenna

No IR Sensor

No Doppler Antenna

Bulged Nose Wheel Door

A Polish Air Force MiG-23UM Flogger C, Red 846, taxies out for another training mission. While all Polish MiG-23MF Flogger B fighters were originally painted in air superiority Gray, a number of them, along with the MiG-23UM trainers, are now camouflaged in a tactical air-to-ground type camouflage.

A Czech Air Force MiG-23UM Flogger C, Black 8325, is towed along the taxiway by a Tatra 138 truck. The instructor's rear cockpit periscope is deployed; however, the aircraft has all its protective covers in place, indicating it is merely being moved to a new parking location.

LTCOL Kriegk (front cockpit) and MAJ Hans Buchanic climb out of an East German Air Force MiG-23UM, Black 100, after a mission in late October of 1980. MAJ Hans Buchanic is commander of one of the three squadrons attached to *Jagdfliegergeschwader 9 Heinrich Rau*.

This MiG-23UM, Black 8109, is being refueled while the crew remains on board. The Flogger C lacks the rear view mirror in the upper canopy framing, as well the two rear view mirrors usually found on the inside canopy framing of fighter MiG-23s.

47

This Hungarian Air Force MiG-23UM, Red 16, at Papa Air Base, once served with the Soviet Air Force before being transferred to Hungary. The Flogger C is equipped with K-13 (AA-2) Atoll air-to-air missile rails on all four pylons. There are only a few Flogger Cs on strength with the *Magyar Legiero* (Hungarian Air Force)

A Polish Air Force MiG-23UM taxies back to its hardstand after a mission. The doors for the braking parachute are open and the instructor's periscope is fully deployed. The camouflaged aircraft in the background are Flogger C trainers while the air superiority Gray aircraft are MiG-23MF Flogger B fighters.

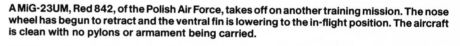

A Soviet MiG-23UM, Red 92, climbs out shortly after takeoff. The nose wheel is fully retracted and the main wheel doors are beginning to close. The aircraft carries no weapons but does have a fuel tank on the centerline pylon.

A MiG-23UM, Red 842, of the Polish Air Force, takes off on another training mission. The nose wheel has begun to retract and the ventral fin is lowering to the in-flight position. The aircraft is clean with no pylons or armament being carried.

With all its protective covers in place, this MiG-23UM, Black 8325, is being towed to a new parking position. The aircraft in the background is an Su-7BMK Fitter A being towed by a Soviet-built URAL truck.

A ground crewman directs a MiG-23UM Flogger C out of its parking spot on the hardstand. The instructor's periscope is fully deployed giving the instructor an improved, but still limited frontal view. The wall behind the aircraft is designed to funnel the engine blast upwards.

A Czech MiG-23UM takes off for a training sortie. The Czech Air Force uses the Flogger C to train both fighter and ground attack pilots. The bright spot under the intake is the starboard retractable landing light.

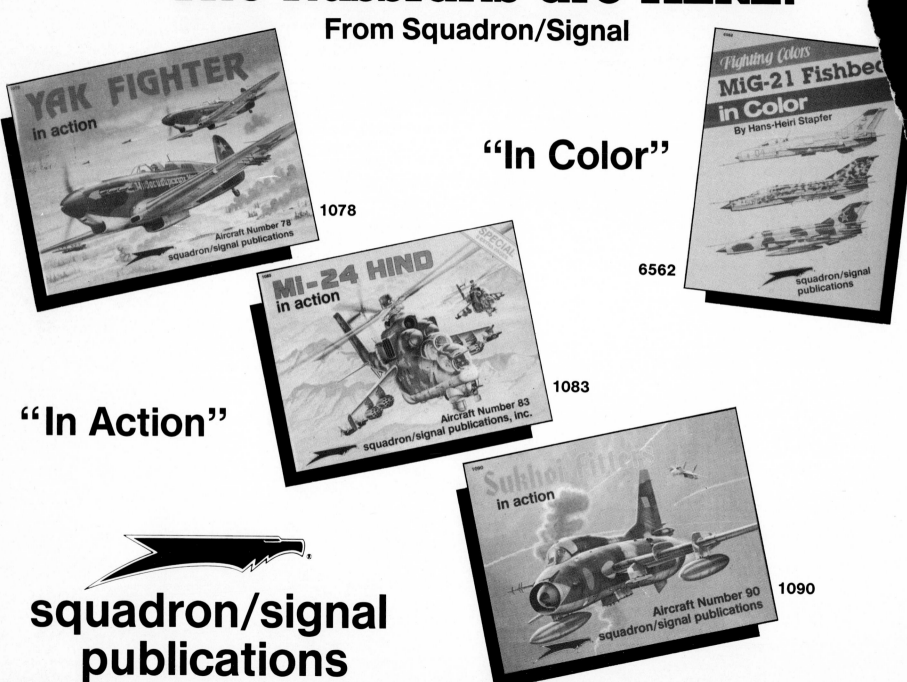

The Russians are HERE!
From Squadron/Signal

"In Color"

"In Action"

squadron/signal publications

1078

1083

6562

1090